MW00588139

Tales From College Football's Sidelines

by
Herschel Nissenson

SPORTS PUBLISHING L.L.C.
WWW.SPORTSPUBLISHINGLLC.COM

Director of Production: Susan M. Moyer
Editor: David Hamburg
Dustjacket and photo insert design: Christina Cary

ISBN:
Hardcover:1-58261-269-2
Softcover:1-58261-327-3

SPORTS PUBLISHING L.L.C.
www.sportspublishingllc.com

Printed in the United States.

For:

—*the four best grandchildren in the world:*
Kody Barrett Young, Madison Paige Young,
Matthew Pierce Arnold and Griffin Scott Arnold;

—*The members of the American Football Coaches Association,*
the greatest guys in the world;

—*And P.T. Barnum, who may have been*
the smartest man who ever lived,
but who vastly underestimated the American public's capacity
for being suckered (example: Dick Vitale).

Contents

Foreword

College Football fans finally have an opportunity to go beyond the sterile press releases and published stories about the coaches, events and other personalities who have dominated the sport.

Herschel Nissenson, the top college football writer, opens his incomparable files, notes and memories to share stories that, for the most part, have not been previously written. And, yes, he tells the incredibly funny, sad and heart wrenching as only he can tell them.

Decades of stories, years of prodding and encouragement to write this book and more years of writing and editing, all for your enjoyment, regardless of your favorite coach, player or team.

Charley Pell
Gadsden, Alabama

Author's Note

I didn't grow up wanting to be a college football writer. Baseball, yes. But my only experience with college football as a child was a game or two at Columbia University's old Baker Field, where everyone stood up for the kickoff and I couldn't see a damn thing.

I played "football" at the City College of New York, but it was called soccer. My main claims to athletic fame are as follows:

I was the backup goalie on the 1954 Metropolitan Soccer Conference champions and was known as the Holy Goalie or Swiss Cheese (take your pick).

My picture used to hang on the wall of CCNY's old Wingate Gym (a team picture).

I was the last cut from tryouts for the CCNY tennis team one year. The tryouts were held indoors, and I had never before played on boards.

I was the manager for the CCNY basketball team one year under legendary coach Nat Holman (after the scandal).

My first job was as a copy boy for International News Service. I was occasionally drafted to fill in on the sports desk when the normal six-man staff, which included a senile columnist and a horse handicapper, was short-handed, which was usually the case.

When INS folded in June 1958, (We were scooped on our own demise by the Dow-Jones ticker), I took a six-month vacation and then spent two years with the *Middletown* (N.Y.) *Daily Record* as telegraph (i.e., world news) editor. The *Daily Record* was the first daily newspaper printed in offset cold type (i.e., no linotype machines). Believe it or not, Middletown, a rather small town less than two hours north of Manhattan, had two daily papers, the upstart *Daily Record*, a real newspaper, and the century-old *Middletown Times Herald*. On the day the Russians sent the first Sputnik into space, the *Times Herald* led with a local woman giving birth to triplets.

In November 1960, two significant events occurred—I got married and went to work for the Associated Press in the Newark (N.J.) bureau. A year later, I became the New Jersey state sports editor and spent the next six years or so covering Rutgers and Princeton football and a lot of college basketball (New Jersey had no professional sports teams, except for a brief fling with the New Jersey Americans of the American Basketball Association).

In February 1968, I was transferred to the New York sports department, which was in the process of delegating beats. The AP had a veteran baseball writer (Joe Reichler) and a well-known pro football writer (Jack Hand), but no college specialists. Ted Smits, the first of five sports editors under whom I worked, told me, "You covered college football in New Jersey. You're the college football guy."

The rest, as Ted Baxter used to say, is history—and what a history it's been.

The AP and I parted company at the end of the 1990 calendar year. I spent the 1991-95 football seasons as a researcher for ESPN and did a little work for CBS-TV in 1997—it must have been very little, since I had been used to working for peanuts ans CBS paid off in peanut shells—when it paid at all.

You will find INS, Middletown, AP, ESPN and CBS tidbits in this book. It's my book, and as such, I can write anything I want to. despite pressure that "you know so many stories," I resisted writing a book for a long time because I was never the kind of writer who set out to hurt anyone. You've heard of a player's coach; I was a coach's writer. There are a few unkind stories in this book and a lot more in my memory, which probably will never be written—at least not by me.

Herschel Nissenson
Freeport, New York

About the author . . .

Herschel Nissenson, a native of New York City, has been a professional journalist for nearly 50 years, including a stint of 20 years as the national college football editor for the Associated Press. In 1982, he was honored by the College Sports Information Directors of America for his contributions to intercollegiate athletics. Herschel and his wife, Amira, live in Freeport, New York, and have three children and four grandchildren.

Dust jacket design: Chrtistina Cary
Front cover photographs: (top left, then clockwise) Paul "Bear" Bryant (AP/Wide World Photos), Eddie Robinson (AP/Wide World Photos), Bo Schembechler (courtesy of University of Michigan), Lou Holtz (AP/Wide World Photos), and Steve Spurrier and Bobby Bowden (AP/Wide World Photos)
Back cover photographs: (top left, then clockwise) Joe Paterno (courtesy of Penn State University), Tom Osborne (Lincoln Journal Star), Woody Hayes (AP/Wide World Photos), Barry Switzer (courtesy of University of Oklahoma)

The Tales

I'm No. 1—Or So I Thought

In 1979, I covered a game between Alabama and LSU in Baton Rouge.

The late Paul Manasseh, LSU's sports information director, made me a reservation at the Baton Rouge Hilton beginning Wednesday night. I was visiting some friends in Birmingham and subsequently decided to arrive on Thursday instead. I informed Paul, but both he and I neglected to inform the hotel.

I flew in early in the morning and arrived at the hotel before 8 a.m., tired and bedraggled. They couldn't find my reservation. The girl at the front desk said, "Let me get the rooms divisions clerk."

She went in back and came out with a pompous-looking fellow who told me, "Yes, I remember your name.

When you didn't arrive by 6 o'clock last night we canceled your reservation."

"Well, here I am," I said. "Uncancel it."

"Well," he said, "I can give you a room for Thursday and Friday nights, but you'll have to leave on Saturday. We're booked solid."

I was beginning to get ticked off.

"Why would I want to do that?" I snapped. "The only reason I'm in this one-horse town is to cover a football game on Saturday night."

I asked for Sandy Something-or-Other, the girl with whom Manasseh had made my reservation.

Mr. Pompous got huffy. "She's not in yet," he said. "And besides, I'm the rooms divisions clerk and I'll give you a room for Thursday and Friday nights, but you'll have to promise to leave on Saturday."

I got huffier. "Well," I said, "I'm the college football editor of the Associated Press and I'll not only promise to leave on Saturday, but I'll promise never again to put LSU in the Top 20 or give you an All-American player. How does that grab you, asshole?"

He squelched me.

"I don't care," he said. "I hate football."

I originally wanted to call this book *Third-and-Three,* for this reason:

You've all heard the old song, "The Girls All Get Prettier at Closing Time." The story goes that the late

Bobby Layne, a famous quarterback and a noted party animal, was in a watering hole that was getting ready to close. There was one woman still around and Layne said, "I'm gonna check her out."

A few minutes later he was back with the following assessment:

"She's worse than third-and-three."

The One And Only Bear

The first time I walked into Bear Bryant's office I was scared shitless.

The Bear sat behind a raised desk like a king on a throne—after all, that's what he was—and his visitor sat on a couch so saggy that your rear end almost scraped the floor and you had to look up at him.

Paul William Bryant was one of only two coaches I didn't address by his first name. Out of respect, I called

Paul (Bear) Bryant (SPI Archives)

him "Coach" rather than "Paul," and I would have felt foolish calling a grown man "Bear." The other coach with whom I didn't get familiar was Woody Hayes, for reasons I'll disclose later on.

Bear Bryant was the subject of my biggest scoop.

It was 9 p.m. on Tuesday, December 14, 1982, and I was in the AP office getting ready to go home.

The phone rang. It was David Housel, then Auburn's sports information director, calling from Orlando, where the Tigers were to play Boston College in the Tangerine Bowl on Saturday, a game I was scheduled to cover. I had a flight to Orlando the next morning.

"I think you ought to hear this," Housel said.

Auburn coach Pat Dye and several members of his staff had Alabama backgrounds. So did New York Giants coach Ray Perkins and several members of his staff. Coaches talk on the phone more than gossipy housewives, and the word the Auburn coaches were getting was that Perkins had told his staff that Bryant was about to retire, with Perkins taking over.

I had to confirm it. But how? I called Bryant's home; the line was busy. This is how it went for the next hour or so—a busy signal at the Bear's house, a call to someone I thought could help, another busy signal and so on.

I reached, among others, Alabama president Dr. Joab Thomas, assistant athletic director (and Bryant lookalike) Sam Bailey, Texas A&M official Charley Thornton (a former Alabama SID and Bryant aide), etc.

Little by little the story came together. The *Washington Post* heard that Perkins was going to spend a year as Alabama's offensive coordinator and then take over.

Finally, I called Logan Young, a Memphis business-man and close friend of Bryant's. His phone didn't answer. Luckily, I had his mother's number. She told me where she thought he was, and the person who answered at that number told me where he really was.

It was news to Logan.

"Let me call Perkins," he said.

Five minutes later, he called me back. Bingo!

"Perkins says it's true," Logan reported.

He gave me Perkins' home number, but Mrs. Perkins said he was in bed and couldn't come to the phone. All my pleading went for naught.

But I had the story down 99 and 44/100s percent. Out of courtesy, I tried Bryant one last time. Amazingly, the line wasn't busy.

Mrs. Bryant answered and we exchanged pleasantries. "Miz Bryant," I said, "I need to talk to Coach and it's real urgent."

"Oh," she said, "he's out recruiting somewhere in Mississippi."

What could I say? I was pretty certain Bryant was home, but I couldn't call Mary Harmon Bryant a liar. I explained that all hell was going to break loose in a few minutes when I put my story on the wire, and I was calling out of friendship and as a courtesy to provide some advance warning.

"Oh," she said, "I'll believe that [the story] when I read it in the papers."

That scared me a little, but not enough to hold the story. I was about to hang up when she said, "You're such a good friend of Paul's. Can't you wait for the press conference in the morning?"

I couldn't. I informed the AP brass what I had and was told those three little words: "It's your career."

The story moved in time for the 11 o'clock news in New York. CBS sportscaster Warner Wolf held up a copy of the wire story and said, "The AP just reported that Bear Bryant will retire in the morning and Ray Perkins will succeed him." Then, he flipped the story over his shoulder onto the floor and said, "Here's what I think of that." The next night he apologized on the air.

By the time I got home it was 4 a.m. I had an 8 o'clock flight to Orlando and I hadn't packed, so I never went to bed. Basically, I held my breath.

The next morning, Alabama held a press conference, and every word of my story was accurate. It was named AP Sports Story of the Year, and I have a plaque to prove it.

The last time I saw the Bear was the day before the 1982 Liberty Bowl, his final game, a 21-15 win over Illinois. I spent some time in his suite at the Holiday Inn Rivermont in Memphis, just me, the Bear and Billy Varner, a University of Alabama security man who served as Bryant's valet.

The Bear reminisced, telling enough great stories to fill a couple of columns. I could listen to the Bear for hours.

I wrote my game story in the press box and wasn't able to get down to the postgame press conference at which Bryant invited the writers to stop by and "break bread" with him if they ever happened to be in Tuscaloosa.

I went from Memphis to the Sugar Bowl, from there to the NCAA convention in San Diego and then to the American Football Coaches Association convention in Los Angeles. The two conventions overlapped some, and by the time I got to L.A., it was the last day of the coaches' meeting. The first person I ran into was Tennessee coach Johnny Majors.

"Where have you been?" he inquired. "Coach Bryant was asking for you, but he's gone home."

When I finally got back to the office, I wrote Bryant a letter saying how much I appreciated all his courtesies over the years and what a pleasure it had been to cover a bunch of Alabama games. I said I not only hoped to break bread with him, but also to take a shot at breaking par on the golf course.

I wrote the letter on a Saturday night and put it in the outgoing mailbox. It went out Monday morning, on Tuesday the Bear took sick and went in the hospital, on Wednesday he died. A few days later my letter came back, unopened, in a University of Alabama envelope with a note saying, "Your letter arrived after Coach Bryant's death. We know you share our sorrow, etc."

I flew down to the funeral. On the plane I scribbled a first-person account of my memories of the Bear. It drew as much reaction as anything I've written. It went like this:

"He smoked too much. If the pocket was Bear Bryant's you could bet it held a crumpled pack of cigarettes.

"He drank too much. When he came to New York a couple of years ago to address the Associated Press Board of Directors, his attaché case contained a bottle of vodka.

"He partied too much. A few Aprils back, when he was hospitalized during spring practice, I asked him what the doctors had diagnosed.

"'They said it was 75 percent smoking, 20 percent diet and 5 percent booze and other stuff,' he replied.

"'I wish,' he added almost wistfully, 'I wish it had been 75 percent of that booze and other stuff.'

"Bear Bryant wasn't a saint. He was a head football coach, for 38 years. He could have coached 38 more and it wouldn't have been too much. 'Too much ain't ever enough,' one of Bryant's 'pupils' once said.

"A letter should have arrived in Bryant's office by now. I mailed it Monday, the day before he entered the hospital. It told the Bear what I somehow neglected to tell him during our last visit, an hour-long private get-together in his Memphis hotel suite the day before his 323rd and last victory.

"It said what a privilege it had been to cover Bryant and Alabama so often, especially during the countdown to his breaking Amos Alonzo Stagg's record of 314 coaching victories.

"I wrote that I intended to take him up on his blanket offer to the media to 'break bread' with him in

Tuscaloosa. Hopefully, I said, we might even try and break par if the torn ligament in his left arm allowed him to swing a golf club.

"The letter will go unanswered now, but I have a feeling Coach Bryant—I could never bring myself to address him as anything other than 'Coach'—will read it, and read between the lines how much he meant to so many of us.

"Oh yes, the Bear knew what the media needed and how to provide it, especially when it served his purpose.

"'Sit down, boy,' he snapped—I was 47 at the time —the day I started to explain that I had planned to be in Tuscaloosa that particular week, long before a story broke in Atlanta charging racial dissension on the Alabama team. 'I'm through tiptoeing around and I'm through pussy-footing around,' he growled. 'I'm going back to being Paul Bryant and anybody who doesn't like the way Paul Bryant does things can get out of here.'

"He went on like that for a while. Then he paused, smiled sheepishly, and said, 'I don't really know what I'm trying to say.'

"Of course, he knew full well what he was doing, giving me a national headline-making story. It even made the *Tuscaloosa News*, Alabama's hometown newspaper.

"Later, Al Browning, the paper's sports editor, told me, 'He told me the same things earlier in the week and said, if I wrote it, he'd kill me.'

"I remember him towering over most people at 6-foot-4, but never looking down on anyone.

"I remember him and John Wayne sitting on the same couch, both slightly smashed.

"I remember he almost ran me over with a golf cart at practice one day, then told me—ordered me—to hop in and asked, 'Do any of those other [blankety-blank] coaches give you this kind of service?'

"I remember him putting his arm around Johnny Majors a few days before the 1976 Pitt-Georgia Sugar Bowl, Majors' last game as Pitt coach before going to Tennessee, and drawling, 'Welcome to the SEC, son.'

"I remember how he never let me forget that in 1966 Alabama was No. 1 in the preseason AP poll, went 11-0 and finished third. It cost him an unprecedented third straight national championship.

"I remember his shuffling along the sidelines, the lined face under the houndstooth hat, the rolled-up program in his hand, scheming up ways to win still another game. And I remember that stretch when the Bear forgot how to 'win the big one' and I covered a half-dozen or more games without seeing Alabama win. 'Shoot,' he would snort, 'are you here again?'

"Those things are all gone now and the Bear's work is done. Ironic how many times his friends used to sit around and wonder if he would ever retire. The consensus was that he would die within a year if he stopped coaching.

"It didn't take that long. There was no spring practice to plan and someone else is on the recruiting trail for Alabama and it was all strange to the Bear. 'This [victory] will make my future years—or year—more pleasant,' he said prophetically after the Liberty Bowl.

"As they said on the farms of Bryant's Arkansas boyhood when the planting was done, the crop has been 'laid by.' And Bear Bryant, who always said he had a plan for everything—a plan for winning and a plan for losing—was left without a plan for coaching. And that left him without any plan at all."

That column drew letters of praise from, among others, Dave Nelson, longtime Delaware coach and secretary of the NCAA's Football Rules Committee, and Syracuse's Dick MacPherson.

It also drew a letter of reprimand from a gentleman in North Carolina who said, "He's not even in the ground and you Yankees can't wait to get on him."

I wrote back and explained what the column really said and suggested the gentleman read it again. A few weeks later he wrote me another letter, saying, "I now see what you really were saying, but at the time I had him on a pedestal and you burst my bubble."

The Bear's funeral was a madhouse. After services in Tuscaloosa, there was a procession to Elmwood Cemetery in Birmingham some 50 miles away. People crowded onto each overpass along Interstate 20 to pay their respects; signs honoring the Bear were draped from each overpass.

Bear Bryant (SPI Archives)

The cemetery was a zoo, with people standing on tombstones and hanging from trees.

I get back to Birmingham every year and I usually visit the Bear's grave and say a few words. I think he hears me, but I won't tell you what I say to him.

When I was there in 1999, I noticed that a tree limb had grown over the Bear's grave. Birds nested in the tree and, birds being birds, there were bird droppings on Bryant's headstone. It didn't seem right.

I don't know if the Bear could walk on water, although, as someone once said, "He sure do know where the stumps are."

They said the Bear could control the weather and I saw him—or some higher authority, although in Alabama there was no higher authority —once do it.

It was a Sugar Bowl in old Tulane Stadium, before the Superdome was built. It poured all day in New Orleans, but when the Alabama team appeared in the tunnel for the pregame warm-up it stopped raining. And it didn't start again until the final gun.

That's when I became a believer.

Ara Parseghian, the former Notre Dame coach, liked to tell the story of the time his team was idle and he was watching a Bama game on TV. An Alabama player went down with an injury. The Bear went out to have a looksee and a few moments later the Alabama player left the field under his own power.

Parseghian said his phone rang and a voice with a Southern accent asked, "Coach Parseghian?"

Ara said yes.

"Coach Parseghian of Notre Dame?"

Ara wondered how many Coach Parseghians there were, at Notre Dame or anywhere else, for that matter.

"Y'all watching the Tide?"

Ara said he was.

"Did y'all see the Beah go out and heal that player?"

⬤

Until he sold it during the summer of 1997, Pat James ran the best barbecue joint in Birmingham. It was so successful that James closed at 5:30 p.m. and didn't even open on weekends.

A strange occupation for someone who played for Bear Bryant at Kentucky, coached for him at Kentucky, Texas A&M and Alabama and later was an assistant coach at LSU and Oklahoma.

Bryant held something close to sainthood status in the coaching fraternity, but he also could be an exasperating boss. James recalls one particular episode at Kentucky. Practice had just ended, and as they walked off the field Bryant said, "I thought Jim Stanley was the best player on the field today."

Said the agreeable James, "I'll go along with that."

Replied Bryant, "I don't give a shit if you go along with it or not."

James said he was so mad, he thought about going home, ordering his wife and kids out of the house, locking himself in a closet and just cussing Bryant for an hour or so.

⬤

There was another time at Kentucky when Bryant petitioned the Southeastern Conference for permission to take about 25 players on a little camping expedition before the official start of fall practice, just to get acquainted. This was a few years before his infamous boot camp at Junction, Texas, when he coached at Texas A&M.

James, then a player, isn't sure if the Bear ever received permission, but that didn't stop him from doing it.

The players lived in open sheds and spent the time fishing and getting to know each other. And, of course, practicing a little. Or maybe a lot. In a field that resembled a cow pasture. In fact, that's what it was.

One day, James went fishing and was late to practice. Bryant didn't say a word until practice was over. Then he said to the team, "One of our players was late to practice today. Pat, I stood up for you, but they held a kangaroo court and decided that you should cover up the cow dung on the field."

James did so with bucket after bucket of sand and dirt.

The next day, Bryant somehow overslept and was late to practice. His teammates all told James he was "chickenshit" if he didn't stand up to the Bear. When practice was over, James said, "Coach Bryant was late to practice today. Coach, I stood up for you, but they held a kangaroo court and decided that you should shovel those cow patties I covered up over the river bank."

Without batting an eye, Bryant did just that.

When Rutgers traveled south in 1981 to meet Alabama in Tuscaloosa, the Scarlet Knights stayed in Bessemer, about 30 miles down the road.

On the morning of the game, Rutgers had a police escort to the game—motorcycles, squad cars, even a helicopter.

"Sure is nice of you to treat us like this," Coach Frank Burns told the bus driver.

Said the driver, "Coach Bryant wants to make sure you show up."

Shortly before Scott Hunter's first start as Alabama's quarterback, Bear Bryant handed him a game program and told him to memorize the names of the officials and to address them by name during the game.

All went well for most of the first half, as Hunter impressed the officials by addressing them as Mr. Jones, Mr. Smith, etc. Late in the half, one of the officials—it may have been George Morris—called pass interference against Alabama and Bryant came ranting off the sideline, yelling, "You no-good thieving Georgia Tech son of a bitch."

Hunter said it didn't matter how he addressed the officials after that.

Bryant equaled Amos Alonzo Stagg's record of 314 wins with a 31-16 victory at Penn State in 1981. There was an injury time-out late in the game.

When Bryant and Joe Paterno arranged the series, they agreed that when the teams played in Alabama they would use SEC officials, with Eastern officials working the games at Penn State.

During the time-out, one of the Eastern officials came over to Bryant and said, "Coach Bryant, I just wanted to tell you how much it means to me to work this game. I always wanted to work one of your games, and I can't tell you what an honor and a privilege it is, especially the game in which you tied Coach Stagg's record."

"We-e-llll," Bryant drawled, "I appreciate that, but I want you to know you screwed us royally."

In 1982, Auburn scored in the closing seconds to beat Alabama 23-22. The fans flooded the gridiron at Legion Field, and clearing them off was going to be an impossible task.

Referee Robert Aillet told umpire Harold Johnson to ask Bryant whether he would agree to cancel the final six seconds.

Said Bryant, "You guys have screwed up this game for 59 minutes and 54 seconds, I guess six more seconds won't make any difference."

●

This one is apocryphal, but a good story nonetheless.

In 1984, Auburn needed to beat Alabama to win the SEC championship and go to the Sugar Bowl. The Tigers trailed 17-15 late in the game and had a fourth-and-goal at the Alabama 1-yard line. Coach Pat Dye decided some divine intervention was needed.

"Lord," he prayed, "I've never been one to ask for help, but here's the situation. If we win, we go to the Sugar Bowl. We can take the lead by kicking a chip-shot field goal, but Alabama has enough time to come back and kick a field goal of their own, and they've already kicked a long one. What should we do?"

"Hold on a second, Pat," the Lord replied. After a pause, the Lord said, "Run Bo Jackson to the right."

Auburn did—and Jackson was stopped cold.

"Lord," Dye implored, "the one time in my life I've ever asked you for help and you let me down. Why did you tell me to run right?"

"Just a second, Pat," the Lord said, and then hollered, "Bear, why'd we tell Pat to run right?"

Bear Bryant was known for covering the spread and keeping his supporters happy.

One year, Bama was a heavy favorite over Southern Mississippi. The Crimson Tide scored with about a minute to go and had a comfortable lead, but hadn't quite covered. So Bryant ordered an onside kick, Alabama recovered, scored and finally covered.

In the Southern Miss locker room, Coach P.W. Underwood spoke to his team. "All right, men," he said, "on your knees; Coach Nix is gonna lead us in the post-game prayer."

Assistant Coach Buddy Nix's prayer went like this: "Lord, don't ever let us get our ass beat this bad again."

Alabama Hall of Famer John Hannah recalls one game in which he made so many mistakes in the first half that Bryant booted him in the rear end—literally—as the teams left the field.

The game was televised and the Hannah family watched it.

Afterward, when Hannah called home looking for a bit of sympathy, his mother wanted to know, "What did you do to make Coach Bryant so mad?"

During the 1980s, I played in a golf outing in Orlando, Florida. I was standing alongside the bus that transported us to the golf course, talking with Pat Jones, then the head coach at Oklahoma State.

Bryant walked up, all agog to tell me how much money he had won on an Arkansas horse—remember, the Bear was from Arkansas—in the Kentucky Derby.

He stuck out his hand to Jones and introduced himself. "Paul Bryant," he said.

"I . . . I . . . I know who you are, Coach," Jones sputtered.

Well, who didn't?

Bill Curry, one of the nicest people in the world but the wrong choice for Alabama, followed Ray Perkins after the Bear retired. If Alabama president Joab Thomas had set out to antagonize Crimson Tide fans, he would have done one of two things—hire a coach with (1) a losing record or (2) with ties to Tennessee, Auburn or Georgia Tech. Thomas did both—Curry had a losing record at his alma mater, Georgia Tech.

Curry, who wouldn't have been accepted by Alabama supporters had he won a national championship every year, took the Crimson Tide back to the Sun Bowl in

1988 to play Army. They won a 29-28 squeaker, thanks to Derrick Thomas, who blocked two field goal attempts.

The game was played the day before Christmas. That night in Montgomery, Alabama, where he was coaching in the Blue-Gray Classic on Christmas Day, Boston College coach Jack Bicknell went to midnight Mass and said he learned how important college football was in the Deep South.

After a lovely service, the celebrants were leaving the church in a beautiful candlelight procession when Bicknell heard someone behind him grumble, "Can you believe the son of a bitch only beat Army by one point!"

Louis Leo Holtz

I first met Lou Holtz in 1973 when his North Carolina State team played Kansas in the Liberty Bowl. Holtz came to New York for a Liberty Bowl press conference in late November—it was the first time in his career he ever missed a practice, he said—at the 21 Club.

Lou Holtz (University of Notre Dame)

Why the Liberty Bowl, which is played in Memphis, Tennessee, had to hold a press conference in New York is anybody's guess, but they did.

The 21 Club is half a block from St. Patrick's Cathedral and Holtz went into the church for a few minutes. When he came out, I asked him if it was worth a touchdown or a field goal. But then I've always been sacrilegious.

I also covered Holtz's Arkansas team against North Carolina in the 1981 Gator Bowl that was played in a dense fog. Holtz, his usual jestful self before the game, which Arkansas lost, said he was surprised to see me "because you only cover good teams."

And that brings us to South Bend, Indiana, home of the University of Notre Dame du Lucre—sorry, du Lac; I forgot that Notre Dame's bolting the CFA for its own TV contract wasn't done for money.

In four decades of covering college football, I came to the conclusion that the worst fans of all belong to Notre Dame.

Now that I've thoroughly antagonized all supporters of the Fighting Irish, let me explain. Notre Dame fans are not loud and crude like some good ol' boys in the South and Southwest. But after covering numerous games in South Bend, it struck me that there is a certain arrogance and snobbishness about them. I got the feeling that they seemed to be saying to the opposition, "You don't realize how lucky you are that we let you come here under the storied Golden Dome and do battle with the hallowed Fighting Irish."

The story I am about to relate started when Lou Holtz left North Carolina State following the 1975 season to become head coach of the New York Jets. I knew Holtz fairly well and, since I live 10 minutes from the Jets' headquarters on Long Island, I dropped him a note welcoming him to town and jokingly telling him to call me if he ever needed a shoulder to cry on. The Jets were coming off a problem-filled season that even Holtz couldn't imagine.

Back came a cute note asking, "Do you have a good strong couch I can come lie down on for a while?"

Jump ahead to the spring of 1989. I went to South Bend to present Notre Dame with the AP national championship trophy. There was a reception at City Hall, then a banquet in the Athletic & Convocation Center attended by several thousand people.

These presentations were an annual rite for me as the AP's college football editor. If I knew the coach pretty well, I needled him some good-naturedly. I told both South Bend gatherings that I was somewhat surprised to see Holtz win a national championship since his Jets act (a 3-10 record) hadn't elicited any rave reviews. I also mentioned our exchange of letters.

Everything went well—or so I thought. I learned differently a couple of months later when I ran into Holtz at a golf outing in Orlando, Florida. At a reception one evening, I went over to say hello. Holtz looked at me and snapped, "I want you to know you went out of your way to embarrass me at our football banquet."

I couldn't believe my ears, but I came up with a snappy reply. "What?" is what I said.

Holtz repeated his statement. I told him I never intended to offend anyone, and didn't think I had. Holtz apparently thought otherwise.

I walked away shaking my head at how many times I had heard Lou Holtz poke fun at himself over his scrawny frame (he was a 155-pound linebacker at Kent State), his slight lisp and other imperfections (he used to claim he was just getting over a case of beriberi).

A few minutes later, I ran into Dick Rosenthal, Notre Dame's athletic director.

"Dick," I said, "you were at the football banquet. Was I out of line?"

"Not that I remember," he answered.

An hour or so later, I came across Gene Corrigan, then commissioner of the Atlantic Coast Conference and Rosenthal's predecessor as Notre Dame AD.

"Hey," said Corrigan, who hadn't even been at the bash in South Bend, "I heard from two people that you were the hit of the Notre Dame football banquet."

Fast-forward to the 1993 season. Notre Dame upset No. 1-ranked Florida State in mid-November, only to lose to Boston College a week later in the regular-season finale.

The Irish recovered to beat Texas A&M in the Cotton Bowl and Holtz began in earnest his campaign for the national championship. So it was then that I decided to do some research.

During the two decades when I tallied the weekly AP college football poll, I learned one thing about the voters—there is no middle ground where Notre Dame is concerned—the voters either love the Irish or hate them.

Whatever, Notre Dame is truly in a league of its own, although it plays as an independent in football. It goes back to the Roaring Twenties, when Grantland Rice immortalized the Four Horsemen and started the country on a love affair with the Irish. Only Notre Dame could double-cross its partners in the College Football Association and negotiate its own TV contract. Only Notre Dame could join a bowl alliance without a conference affiliation.

I have nothing against Notre Dame personally. Ara Parseghian was as fine a man who ever lived.

Gerry Faust? Don't ever knock Gerry Faust in my presence. In 1985, I was supposed to cover the USC-Notre Dame game and had an appointment with Faust. However, my mother was diagnosed with cancer and everything was off.

A handwritten note arrived on Faust's personal stationery with the "JMJ" monogram. It read: "I went to the Grotto (a religious shrine on the Notre Dame campus) and lit a candle for your mother."

If you want to blame anyone for Faust's 30-26 record at Notre Dame, blame the Rev. Edmund Joyce, who hired him from Moeller High School in Cincinnati. It was too big a jump, much too big.

That brings us to 1993 and the research I mentioned earlier. I concluded that Holtz may have had a point about the 1993 national championship, but here's what I learned about Notre Dame's other national crowns:

—In 1943, Notre Dame lost its final game and remained No. 1, the only time this has happened in the history of the AP poll.

—In 1946, No. 2 Notre Dame played the famous 0-0 tie with No. 1 Army and remained No. 2, then somehow jumped the unbeaten Cadets (27-0-1 over three seasons) four weeks later in the final poll after Army struggled to beat an unseaworthy Navy team 21-18.

—In 1947, Notre Dame was unbeaten and untied, but so were Michigan and Penn State, two passably good football schools. In fact, the AP held a special two-team post-bowl unofficial poll after Michigan beat Southern Cal 49-0 in the Rose Bowl (Notre Dame didn't go bowling in those days, but beat USC 38-7 during the regular season) and Michigan won handily.

—In 1949, Notre Dame was unbeaten and untied, but so were Oklahoma, California and Army, not exactly fly-by-night programs.

—In 1966, Notre Dame remained No. 1 despite the infamous 10-10 battle with No. 2 Michigan State. Alabama went 10-0-0 and finished third, a team Bear Bryant always claimed was the best he ever had. Remember, Bryant won five national championships.

—In 1973, Notre Dame won fair and square by defeating Alabama in the Sugar Bowl on a missed PAT. But the Irish wouldn't have won the national championship if the voting had been done on a regular-season basis, which it was until 1968, except for a one-year trial run after the bowls in 1965.

—In 1977, Notre Dame won again despite losing to a 6-5 Ole Miss team that never appeared in the rankings all season. Luckily, Notre Dame got to play No. 1 Texas in the Cotton Bowl, won handily and jumped from fifth to first over an Alabama team that came into the bowls No. 3 and hammered Ohio State 35-6 in the Sugar Bowl, the only time Bear Bryant and Woody Hayes squared off.

—In 1988, Notre Dame won out thanks to a controversial 31-30 win over Miami, a game in which Miami committed seven turnovers and got a terrible call on a "fumble" at the Notre Dame 1-yard line that cost the Hurricanes a touchdown. The game was decided when Miami went for a two-point conversion and missed with 45 seconds left. Had the Hurricanes kicked the point and tied, Notre Dame would not have won the national championship.

I also researched some Notre Dame Heisman Trophies. Angelo Bertelli won the 1943 Heisman despite playing in just six games (he went into the Marine Corps in mid-season). In 1956, Paul Hornung became the only Heisman winner from a losing team (the Irish were 2-8). Hornung didn't even have the most first-place votes.

Tim Brown won the 1987 Heisman by returning two punts for touchdowns against Michigan State in an early-season TV game. Brown did have some "fantastic" numbers that year; he caught 39 passes for 846 yards and three touchdowns, returned 23 kickoffs for 456 yards and a 19.8 average (lowest at Notre Dame in a nine-year stretch) and returned 34 punts for 401 yards, an 11.8-

yard average (Barry Sanders led the nation with a 31.6 average).

I wrote all this in a column. Two months later, I bumped into Holtz again. "Someone sent me a copy of that column you wrote," he snapped. Then he turned on his heel and stalked away.

I didn't even get a chance to ask him if he liked it.

Although I had no occasion to converse with Holtz for a few years, we did shake hands, albeit accidentally, at the annual Hall of Fame banquet in New York in December 1993.

I was wandering around, "working" the room, when I passed the Notre Dame table. Sitting at the end was George Kelly, a longtime coach and member of the athletic department.

We shook hands and George said, "Have you seen Coach?"

Holtz was at the other end of the table and was looking the other way. I tried to get away, but Kelly was persistent.

"Coach," he shouted, "look who's here."

Lou came over and I told him again that I hadn't meant to offend anyone in my 1989 South Bend appearance. Holtz put his hand over his heart as though he was preparing to recite the Pledge of Allegiance and said, "You have no idea how deeply you hurt me."

Nevertheless, we parted on good terms. Holtz even greeted me warmly at the annual Southeastern Conference pre-media days in 1999 before his first season at South Carolina.

I even wrote the following two columns during the fall of 1999. The first one deals with his humorous side, the second looks at his serious side.

Column No. 1:

With a 1-10 record, South Carolina's 1998 football team was no laughing matter. Enter Louis Leo "Leave 'Em Laughing Lou" Holtz. It remains to be seen if Holtz will be funnier than his team.

A noted magician, Holtz didn't do his newspaper or rope tricks at the Southeastern Conference media days in late July, but his routine brought down the house anyway.

Holtz left a cushy TV job for South Carolina, so the logical first question was, "Why did you get back in coaching?"

"A psychiatrist asked me the same thing prior to inducting me into the psycho ward," Holtz quipped.

The 62-year-old Holtz, two years removed from Notre Dame, will need all the legerdemain at his disposal (after all, he took William & Mary to the 1970 Tangerine Bowl with a 5-6 record) at a school where the football tradition consists of one Heisman Trophy (George

Rogers, 1980) and one 10-win season (1984). South Carolina has won only one of nine bowl games and is one of the few state universities that isn't the dominant team in its own backyard (see arch-rival Clemson). Holtz, on the other hand, has been to 20 bowl games with four different teams.

"I tried to buy our way out of nine games," Holtz said. "Nine-and-two'd be okay . . . not that we could win the other two."

Surely Holtz was aware that South Carolina must play SEC East Division rivals Tennessee, Florida and Georgia EVERY year.

"I heard (Tennessee's) Phillip Fulmer talk about how tough the Eastern Division was and I had to chuckle when I heard him say that because he has to play us and doesn't have to play himself," Holtz said.

Holtz's love of running the football and the option has been well documented. He is one of those coaches who think three things can happen when you throw the ball and two of them are bad. Don't expect him to change.

"My son [Skip, the offensive coordinator] loves to throw the football," Holtz said. "He threw for 290 yards a game [as head coach] at Connecticut and he'll call the plays until we throw 11 passes and then I'll call them."

Holtz has raised fan interest in a program which has rarely lacked for support. But can South Carolina even compete with Vanderbilt and Kentucky, much less the division's big three?

"In all honesty, winning the national championship would have to be considered a good season," Holtz says. "We want to win every football game, but the difficulty is our schedule. We play Tennessee and Georgia, we play Tennessee and Florida and Clemson back-to-back. I said to Dr. [Athletic Director Mike] McGee, 'How much do we get to play Tennessee and Florida?' He told me. I said, 'That won't cover hospital bills.'"

Holtz brought his sharp repartee and variety of needles to Columbia.

"I was breaking down the (1998) Florida game, Boo Williams carried the ball three times for two yards. I said to him, 'Were you tired after the Florida game?' He said, 'Not necessarily.' I said, 'I hope not, carrying three times.'

"You know, Boo ran a forty in 4.28. He said, 'Hey, Coach, I ran a 4.28.' I said, 'I didn't know the football was that heavy.' He says, 'What do you mean?' I said, 'You don't run a 4.28 on the field.'"

Nobody from South Carolina was selected in the April NFL draft. Holtz promises that will change.

"I told Boo and [defensive back] Arturo Freeman, 'We'll have five players drafted.' They got all excited. I said, 'Two by the Army, one by the Air Force.'"

South Carolina needs improvement everywhere, but especially on pass defense. The Gamecocks intercepted only five passes all last season. Even Holtz can't win without players.

"[Tennessee's] Tee Martin completed 23 passes in a row against us last year," Holtz noted. "We can't complete 23 in a row without a defense. And it takes a rare individual to be a cornerback. They spread 'em out, there's 87 people and they say, 'Cover him,' and you're looking at a long distance phone call to the next closest defender and then you find out [the receiver] runs 4.2 and you run 4.9 and the coach says, 'Don't let him catch a quickout, but don't get beat deep.'"

Holtz returned to South Bend for a testimonial for the Rev. Theodore Hesburgh, former Notre Dame president.

"They asked me to speak to the students. They asked about my wife [Beth Holtz has been suffering from throat cancer] and I said, 'If she keeps gaining weight, I promised her I'm gonna take her to the Holy Land.' They said, 'That's great coach. We're so excited you're gonna bring her back to Notre Dame.'"

South Carolina's first two games were on ESPN.

"One of the first questions they asked me was, 'Why do you think South Carolina's on national television when you went 1-10 [in 1998]?' They wanted me to say it's because I'm there. I said, 'Obviously they're trying to reduce the amount of violence on TV.'"

The time has come for Holtz to put the one-liners in the garage with his golf clubs for the season and get serious.

Column No. 2:

Lou Holtz was in Nashville last year (1998) preparing for an NFL game on CBS-TV when he was talked into returning to coaching.

"My wife called and said, 'South Carolina called and I think you ought to reconsider. I just think it's some-

Lou Holtz (University of Notre Dame)

thing you ought to do,'" Holtz said. "She said, 'I've talked to Skip [Holtz's son, then head coach at the University of Connecticut] and Skip'll come.'"

Since leaving Notre Dame after the 1996 season because, as he put it, "It was the right time," Holtz had turned down several offers to get back into coaching. But Beth Holtz's remarks got him thinking.

Beth Holtz had stage four throat cancer. She underwent 12 hours of lifesaving surgery at the Mayo Clinic

35

and 83 radiation treatments. She has no saliva glands, no taste buds and her weight had dropped from 129 pounds to 89. Her survival chance was 10 percent.

So when she said she wanted Holtz back in coaching at a school he had turned down three times, a school which hit rock-bottom at 1-10 last year, it raised a question.

"What went through my thought was, 'Does she know something I don't know and she wants to make sure that if something happens to her that I am not alone?'" Holtz said. "I started to wonder about that. But when we talked about it, I think she could tell that I'm happiest when I'm a teacher. That's all I am. That was the main thing."

Another consideration was South Carolina's relative proximity to Beth Holtz's oncologist at the University of Florida's Shands Hospital in Gainesville. Beth Holtz is making good progress and this is one time a husband won't catch hell for disclosing his wife's weight, which is back over 100 pounds and rising.

"I did have many opportunities, and many of them were wonderful jobs," Holtz said. "But I would never allow my wife to go for her checkup without me being there because if something were to go wrong, I'd want to be there. I don't want her to ever call me and tell me on the phone. She called me from the doctor's office the first time she was diagnosed. I said I'll never let that happen again.

"So the fact that we would not have to change doctors, the fact that it's in a great conference, the fact it was a tremendous challenge, the fact that I think South Carolina's a wonderful place to live.

"If you have to live one place year-round, South Carolina's a good place to live weather-wise. It's beautiful, you got the ocean, you got the mountains, you got interest, you got support, but also because of the challenge. I felt maybe we could make a difference.

"There were many other better jobs. I heard many coaches in this conference say don't go to South Carolina, you can't win there. There's better jobs you can go to. There are a lot of people who don't think we can win at South Carolina."

Holtz isn't one of them, although he isn't promising a quick fix.

"This is the sixth situation I've inherited, and I've never taken over a winner [even Notre Dame was 5-6 the year before Holtz arrived]. But this is probably the most difficult because of the schedule we play and the lack of success we've had tradition-wise.

"Every place I've been you had something to build on. At South Carolina we have a lot of assets. I am totally convinced we can be successful in the long range, but I'm not a young man (he's 62), I'm not on an eight-year rebuilding program. We want to win as soon as possible.

"The few talents I have are better suited for working with young people. I loved working with CBS . . . but I didn't feel I was making a difference. I think what life's all about is being able to make a difference in people's lives. I turned the [South Carolina] job down three different times and I finally accepted it because Dr. [Athletic Director Mike] McGee and Dr. [University President John] Palms felt that the situation was such that I could make a difference.

"I'm not here to prove anything. I don't think I have anything to prove. If I haven't done it in 28 years as a head coach, I'm not gonna prove it now. I'm not here to do anything except try to make South Carolina a winner and build a sound program for our coaches and for our players.

"But that was the main thing —I'm a teacher, that's all I do. I felt that if I never coached again, people would say, 'He's always been associated with Notre Dame,' and that would have been a great way to be remembered. My wife and I prayed on it and we decided this—God's more interested in helping me utilize the talents and abilities I have and how I'll be remembered by doing something. I didn't think I'd ever coach again when I left Notre Dame. Where do you go from Notre Dame except straight to heaven and sit by the Pope? That's what my mother said."

With Tennessee, Florida and Georgia in the same SEC division, Holtz knows any promises would be foolish. He has seen too many coaches fail to live up to their predictions.

"I've never made a promise we're gonna win," he says. "The only thing I promise is we aren't gonna forfeit. I do make this commitment—we can win at South Carolina. We can be an excellent football team. I cannot tell you how long it'll take us, but . . . our mandate is to make sure that everybody around the country understands that we have a commitment to excellence at South Carolina.

"I am a fundamentalist. I believe in blocking, I believe in tackling, I believe in the brush block on offense, I believe in brushing their chest up against their spine. I don't think there's anything real complicated about it.

"We aren't gonna win 'cause I'm here any more than you're gonna change a flat tire by changing the driver. If I do have a talent, it's my ability to get people to come together and accept their obligations and their responsibilities.

"Don't think we're gonna give up on this season or say we can't win. I've never gone into a game where I didn't believe we could win. I don't believe there's a problem in this world that there's not an answer or a solution. There's an answer to every problem we have on our football team. The question is are we gonna be able to find the answers?"

In the 1980s, Notre Dame was recruiting a hotshot prep quarterback named Billy Ray. It looked like Ray was going to Alabama—he did, and later transferred to Duke —so Holtz decided to step in at the last minute.

"Son," he told Ray on the phone, "I want you to know I was the first coach in Arkansas history to play a black quarterback."

Ray thought that one over and then informed Holtz, "Coach, I'm not black."

Pete Cordelli spent 14 years under Holtz as a player and coach at North Carolina State, Arkansas and Notre Dame.

Arkansas, a huge underdog—and despite the suspension of a few frontline players—upset Oklahoma 31-6 in the Orange Bowl to cap the 1977 season and Cordelli tells the following story:

"We lost not only the three players for the suspension (Donny Bobo, Micheal (CQ) Forrest, Ben Cowins), but also lost Leotis Harris, who was an All-American guard. So you lose 80 percent of your offensive firepower with the three skill guys and then you lose your best offensive lineman and the game goes off the board in Vegas. It had gotten to 24 points and then they finally pulled it.

"There were some questions whether some of the players were going to show up in Miami after what happened in Fayetteville.

Well, Coach has a meeting and he says just make sure everybody shows up.

"So we assemble in Miami on Christmas Day and we have a team meeting and he said to the team, 'You people don't understand everything that went on in Fayetteville 'cause most of you were gone. But I'm gonna give you an opportunity to leave. Whoever wants to leave, you have three minutes. Myself and the coaches, we're walking out. As soon as I walk out that door you have three minutes. If you want to go, get up and get out, and whoever stays, we'll still win the game. And if anybody stands up to leave, I don't want anybody trying to talk 'em out of it. Don't convince anybody that they have to stay if they don't want to.'

"So the coaches get outside. There's conversation going on, you can hear it through the door. Three minutes are up, he walks back in, 'All right, sit down, here's the way it's gonna be.' And he launches into this tirade for about 30 minutes, he reads the riot act, he says, 'That's it. Just make your minds up we're gonna beat Oklahoma.'

"Practice doesn't go very well for about the first three or four days. Guys are still questioning whether they should be there or not. We get into the locker room before the game and the one thing that Coach had never done in all the bowl games that he'd ever participated in, he'd never played in the rain before.

"We're driving to the stadium and it's pouring, absolutely pouring. We get a hell of a thunderstorm. We get out on the field, the field was wet, it's still drizzling, we come back in and he's setting his watch based on the Rose Bowl (TV was contractually obligated to show the Rose Bowl in its entirety).

"As soon as the Rose Bowl was over we were going on the field to start the game. So he looks at his watch and says, 'It's time.' He walks in. Being around him for 14 years, he gives the best pregame talk I'd ever heard him give. When I was at N.C. State as a player, he gave us a great one before we beat Penn State. But this was the best by far.

"And he concludes it by saying, 'In 15 seconds there's gonna be a knock on that door, that's gonna be the official coming in here to get us. Get up, get ready and let's go get Oklahoma. And sure enough, as soon as he said it —Boom! Boom! Boom!—there's a knock on the door, the official walks in, everybody runs up.

"The official says, 'Coach, we have a problem.' Lou says, 'What?' Guys are banging into one another 'cause we're expecting to run out. The Rose Bowl was running late; they said you gotta wait for another 15 minutes.

"'Fifteen minutes? Do you understand I just gave the best pregame speech of my life and now you're trying to screw me up.'

"The official doesn't know what he's talking about. He said, 'Coach, I don't control TV. I'll come back and get you in 15 minutes.'

"So now he has to turn around. We were at a fever pitch, ready to go. So the players go back and sit down and the coaches go back who were gonna be on the sideline because the other coaches had already gone up to the press box thinking the game was gonna be on time.

"We come back as a group of coaches and we're sitting in the coaches' room. He says, 'What am I gonna do? Our guys are in there ready to go. It's like when you ball your hand up in a fist. They're getting tighter and tighter.'

"So he looks at Kiffin and he says, 'Monte, what am I gonna do?'

"He [Kiffin] is sitting over there chain-smoking. He says, 'Coach, I don't know, I don't know what to tell you.'

"So he's pacing back and forth, and this is one of the things that made Lou so good, he was so quick on his feet. Finally, he says, 'I got it.' He says, 'All right, guys, listen, we got a little time. As you know, I go around the country giving a lot of speeches, but my material's getting real old. If anybody in this room can give me an impersonation or a joke I can use . . . we'll go back and forth. You give me one, I'll give you one.'

"Dan Hampton is sitting there on the floor, he looks at me and he says, 'Has he lost his mind? What's he doing?'

"I said, 'Man, go along with it.' He said, 'We're getting ready to play Oklahoma and he wants to tell jokes. What the hell.'

"Guys are looking around, they didn't know if he was serious or not. We had a punter from St. Louis name of Bruce Lahay. Lahay raises his hand and says, 'Coach, I got one for you.'

"He said, 'All right, Lahay, go ahead. It would figure that a damn kicker would be the first guy to come up with something like that.'

"He told the worst joke anybody had ever heard. 'My God, Lahay, I should throw you off scholarship for that.' But everybody starts laughing and it's exactly what he wanted to do.

He just wanted to break the tension, get everybody relaxed.

"So now he tells a joke, then somebody else tells a joke and it goes around and around. All of a sudden everybody's kinda loosening up. All of a sudden the official walks in and says, 'Coach, it's time.' He [Holtz] said, 'Guys, I got nothing else to say. Let's go kick their ass.'

"So we get on the field, third play of the game Oklahoma fumbles and we go in and score. Hold 'em the next series, it's 14-0. The third time we get the ball—when the game started, the rain stopped. Everybody's like, 'Ohmigod, can you believe this?'

"The third series we had the ball, he would pace and I'd have to get the play and send it to the press box to Don Breaux and to Jesse Branch. He's wearing a sweater, do you remember how humid it was that night? First down we gain like two yards, so now he calls a trap option, we're on about the 40-yard line, [Ron] Calcagni's the quarterback, who was a pretty good runner. It's supposed to be coming right and Mark Lewis is the right guard, Jerry Sullivan's the left guard. Lewis pulls, Sullivan pulls, there's a hell of a collision, they knock each other down, we lost eight. Lou remains calm.

"So now, rather than being second-and-eight it's third-and-16. He walks over to Larry Beightol and he puts his arm around him and he says, 'Coach Beightol, can you tell us what happened on that play?'

"Well, Beck's so intense and everything, he said, 'That asshole Lewis went the wrong goddamn way. How stupid . . .'

"Lou jumps back and says, 'Hey, Beck, quit cussin' because I've got this microphone on for NBC.'

Now he [Beightol] starts yelling at Lou, 'You son of a bitch.' They start arguing with each other. Beck says, 'You didn't tell us you were wearing that microphone on the sideline.' We get a delay of game penalty because those two are arguing over the microphone.

"A year later we go to the Fiesta Bowl to play UCLA, we ended up tying 'em 10-10. The morning of the game we always had a staff meeting real quick to go over some last-minute deals. Lou says, 'Anybody have any questions?'

"Beightol says, 'Yeah, you gonna wear that goddamn microphone again for TV?'

"He said, 'What if I do?'

"He says, 'You can kiss my ass on the 50-yard line, Row Z. Don't talk to me again.'"

Another Cordelli story, this one at Notre Dame:

"There was a player at Notre Dame that had come in from Chicago, but was dismissed from school and ended up transferring to Michigan State [Jeff Pearson]. Pearson had made some comments in the paper about Notre Dame he really shouldn't have, it was a little out of line for him to do that.

"Lou took some offense to it, and he should have, because Pearson took some shots that were uncalled for. Pearson was lucky the truth hadn't come out why he was dismissed from Notre Dame, but that's another story for another time.

"He transfers to Michigan State and sits out a year, and the week he becomes eligible, he makes some statements. The *Chicago Tribune* picks up on it. It's big news. Lou had mentioned the one thing he didn't want to have happen was Pearson say some things. It turned ugly.

"Before the game, you know how the coaches meet during warm-ups, talk, whatever coaches do before a game. Lou was a little incensed by these comments and he walked up to [Michigan State coach George] Perles and he started poking George, 'I can't believe that you let Pearson do this.'

"It didn't get real far when Perles grabbed his finger and told him what he would do with it if he continued to poke him with it and proceeded to speak to him not exactly in the King's English.

"Lou took off and went back to the dressing room. He just was shocked, in a panic that George Perles would even talk to him this way, that George threatened to whip his ass. He was just visibly, visibly upset. 'I can't believe the guy would even say that to me.'

"George had a great effect on Lou's mental state before that game. Thank God for Timmy Brown [two punt returns for touchdowns]."

There is no love lost between Holtz and Mississippi State's Jackie Sherrill. A few weeks after Sherrill's Texas A&M squad beat Holtz and Notre Dame 35-10 in the January 1, 1988, Cotton Bowl, they were rival head coaches in the Japan Bowl All-Star Game.

With a few seconds left to play, Sherrill's team had a two-touchdown lead and was threatening to score again. Sherrill called time out to attempt a last-second pass. ESPN was televising the game. Afterward, analyst Lee Corso sought out an old friend, San Diego State coach Denny Stolz, who was serving as Sherrill's offensive coordinator, to ask what had happened.

"All I can tell you," Stolz reported, "is that with one minute to play, Jackie became his own offensive coordinator."

The King of Oklahoma . . . and Jimmy Jump-Up

First of all, let me say it is a disgrace that Barry Switzer is not in the College Football Hall of Fame. Terry Donahue is and Barry Switzer isn't? What's going on here?

It was long overdue, but Barry Switzer has finally been elected to College Football's Hall of Fame. (SPI Archives)

Barry Switzer's first year as a head coach was 1973. The Oklahoma Sooners went 10-0-1, and the tie was on the road at defending national champion Southern California.

The next year, the Sooners went 11-0 and won the national championship, although they were on probation and didn't go to a bowl game.

In 1975, Oklahoma won its first eight games, making Switzer's record a near-perfect 29-0-1. Finally came a loss, 23-3 to Kansas. The *Oklahoma City Times* received a phone call from an angry fan, obviously spoiled by the Sooners' 47-game winning streak in the Bud Wilkinson era, who growled, "I told 'em when they hired the son of a bitch he'd lose a game every couple o' years."

That loss plummeted Oklahoma from second to sixth in the AP poll, and a hard-earned 28-27 win over Missouri on a two-point conversion dropped the Sooners to seventh. But they rose to third with a 35-10 defeat of Nebraska and won a second straight national championship by beating Michigan 14-6 in the Orange Bowl while No. 1 Ohio State lost its bowl game and No. 2 Texas A&M lost its final regular-season game as well as its bowl game.

Michigan's only touchdown came after the Wolverines recovered a fumble on the Oklahoma 2-yard line.

"I hope the voters don't hold Michigan's two-yard scoring drive against us," defensive coordinator Larry Lacewell said.

The voters didn't. The Chinamen probably did.

Say what? Chinamen?

Yes, those rabid and crazy Sooner fanatics, like the guy with the Oklahoma red teeth, for whom too much ain't ever enough, were known to Oklahoma insiders as Chinamen. Seems the Sooners once had the audacity to beat Kansas State by "only" 42-7, or something like that (this was during K-State's futile period), and a caller to the Oklahoma City paper griped, "What's our program coming to when we can't beat Kansas State by more than 42-7, etc., etc."

The writer who fielded the call finally hung up and said, "How much rice can a Chinaman eat?"

Barry Switzer always wore the black hat where the media was concerned. Switzer wasn't a choir boy, but his reputation was largely undeserved.

If you were Barry Switzer's friend, you were a friend for life, and Switzer was as loyal a friend as anyone could want.

When Jimmy Johnson left the University of Pittsburgh to take the head job at Oklahoma State, I told him, "You're the luckiest S.O.B. that ever lived."

"Why?" he asked.

"Because you're the wildest horse rider to ever come down the pike and no one out there will even know you're alive."

It was true. If Switzer sneezed, it made headlines.

Every time I visited Switzer's office, the first question he asked was, "What's the public perception of our program?"

"Barry," I usually said, "they think you're a bunch of crooks. (Pause.) Aren't you?"

After another pause, we'd both laugh.

On Sunday mornings Switzer would fly from Norman to Tulsa—a hop, skip and jump by plane—to do his TV show. One Sunday, Oklahoma was fogged in. Switzer got an urgent call, hopped in his car and headed for Tulsa, a drive of several hours.

En route, he was stopped by a state trooper. When the cop realized who was driving, he said, "Hey, Coach, you were going pretty fast. I'll let it go this time, but it's a good thing you beat Texas' ass yesterday."

One year, Bear Bryant filed a lawsuit against the NCAA's attempt to cut coaching staffs. Switzer was asked to predict the outcome.

"Let me get this straight," he said. "Bear Bryant is suing the NCAA in an Alabama court where the judge is a graduate of the University of Alabama Law School? Don't ask me who's going to win or lose, just give me the point spread."

Barry Switzer and Tom Osborne not only were archrivals, but archopposites. They weren't enemies and got along well, but two more different personalities would be hard to find. I always said Osborne was miscast working for fun-loving Nebraska athletic director Bob Devaney. Switzer and Devaney would have been a perfect couple.

Tom Osborne's record in 25 seasons as Nebraska's head coach was 255-49-3 for a winning percentage of .836. Against Switzer, however, he was 5-12. Subtract those games from his overall record and Osborne would be 250-37-3—.867, a percentage surpassed only by Notre Dame's Knute Rockne (105-12-5—.881).

Oklahoma's wishbone offense in the 1970s was as potent a ground attack as football has ever seen.

The day before the 1974 Oklahoma-Colorado game in Boulder, Bill Mallory, in his first year as Colorado's head coach, was asked if he thought his Buffaloes could slow down the Sooners' ground assault. Mallory never missed a beat. "We saw the wishbone when I coached at

Miami of Ohio," he said, "and we had no trouble stopping it."

I remember thinking, "Welcome to the big time, Coach."

Final score: Oklahoma 49, Colorado 14 . . . and it wasn't that close.

North Carolina had a pretty good team in 1980. It was Lawrence Taylor's senior year and midway through the season the Tar Heels were unbeaten and ranked No. 6 nationally.

I covered Carolina's 28-8 win over North Carolina State, and the folks in Chapel Hill were pretty giddy. As we left Kenan Stadium, one of Carolina's athletic people said to me, "You know, we get a hell of a break because in two weeks we have to go out and play Oklahoma, but next week we play East Carolina, and they run the wishbone just like Oklahoma."

Dick Crum (University of North Carolina)

I signaled for a time-out and said, "They line up in the wishbone just like Oklahoma. You may notice a slight difference when they run the option pitch and turn the corner."

Final score? Oklahoma 41-7. And it wasn't that close.

That was the game when Switzer kept referring to North Carolina coach Dick Crum as "Denny."

Oklahoma won the 1985 national championship by defeating Penn State in the Orange Bowl. But in practice sessions leading up to the game, the Sooners were so short of quarterbacks, they had to press Mike Clopton into service to help out with what passed—that's a pun—for their passing game.

Clopton had been a junior college All-American quarterback who lettered for Oklahoma in 1983, but was then an intern in the business office.

He never played much for the Sooners after undergoing rotator cuff surgery during his junior college days. Switzer, unaware of the surgery, information which wasn't volunteered by Clopton, recruited Clopton by promising him the Sooners were going to throw the football more often. Of course, they didn't.

Switzer told me with an evil grin, "He lied to us, we lied to him."

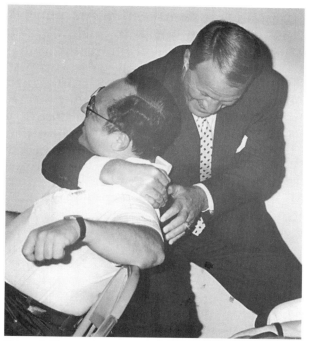

Hopefully, Barry Switzer was only hoping to become a rassler like former Oklahoma footballer Wahoo McDaniel when he used me for target practice. I hope the smile was for real. (Photo courtesy of Herschel Nissenson)

I consider Barry Switzer such a good friend that when he ran afoul of the law in DFW Airport by having a gun in his carry-on luggage, I resisted the temptation to call and sing him a line from an old Gene Autry song that goes, "Ridin' the range once more, totin' my old forty-four."

Wendell Mosley coached Oklahoma's running backs in 1972-75 and 1979-81, which means he coached some truly great ones, including Little Joe Washington, whom he recruited out of Port Arthur, Texas.

Mosley was the butt of numerous jokes and pranks. The Mosley story I like best concerns wide receiver Tinker Owens, who was putting on a show at practice one day, making all sorts of fancy catches.

Switzer was watching Owens' antics and commented, "Wendell, that Tinker Owens sure has charisma, doesn't he?"

"Yeah," Mosley agreed, "but I think he'll be ready to play by Saturday."

That brings me to Jimmy Johnson. I was in Dallas at the American Football Coaches Association's annual golf deal in June 1984 when Howard Schnellenberger resigned as coach at the University of Miami.

I spotted Johnson in deep discussion with Sam Jankovich, the Miami athletic director. "If people see you two together, rumors are going to start flying," I said.

"What's wrong with that?" Johnson replied.

So I knew he was serious about the Miami job, and it became more than a suspicion when Jankovich pumped me for information about Johnson.

That night, a bunch of us went to dinner. Afterward, Johnson and I sat in the hotel lounge until the wee hours, and I tried to talk him out of going to Miami. I mentioned that the university had appropriated $1 million from the 1983 Orange Bowl payoff for the university's general fund, I said that President Tad Foote was somewhat eccentric, I said that Miami's 1983 national championship was a fluke (shows you how much I knew) and that the Hurricanes realistically should always be No. 3 in the state behind Florida and Florida State —or Florida State and Florida.

Jimmy Johnson
(Oklahoma State University)

I was concerned that Johnson was going for the City of Miami and not for the football program because he kept telling me, "I want to live in a big city with a beach." I finally told him, "Go coach at Galveston Ball High School."

Gil Brandt, the former personnel guru of the Dallas Cowboys, said I was responsible for the best comeback line he ever heard. That's the same Gil Brandt who once showed up for the Florida Citrus Bowl's annual golf tournament claiming a 26 handicap and proceeded to shoot a 77; that's a net 51 if you're scoring.

One year, I was paired with another 'D' player and two 'C' players. We never birdied a single hole and shot an 80 at Arnold Palmer's Bay Hill course.

The booby prize, awarded to each member of our foursome, actually was something to cherish—a broken golf club mounted on a piece of driftwood. It hangs proudly on the wall above my desk.

As I returned from the podium to my seat carrying my plaque, Johnson, then the head coach at Oklahoma State, called out, "How high was your score?"

My rapid retort: "Not as high as Nebraska scored on you (actually that was only 54-7)."

Once I played with Johnson in a cutthroat golf deal called the Blackjack Invitational at the Stillwater (Oklahoma) Country Club. The eighth hole is a par 4 that doglegs right around a grove of trees. The perfect drive would be to cut the left corner of the trees, which is what I tried to do.

I hit the hell out of the ball. Unfortunately, I also pulled it. I say unfortunately because (1) I happen to play golf left-handed and (2) I had no idea what was behind the trees.

The ball soared dramatically, up, up and away over the trees. The first sound was Johnson saying, "Oh-oh"; the next was the tinkle of breaking glass.

We hopped in the cart and drove around the trees to find a lady standing on her second-floor patio holding a golf ball between thumb and forefinger.

"We've lived in this house for 11 years," she said, "and we've had a lot of balls come bouncing off the roof, but this is the first one that's ever come through our sliding plate-glass window."

Shoot, even Tiger Woods doesn't hit them straight all the time, does he? If I lived alongside a golf course, I'd have unbreakable window glass. Wouldn't you?

Nissenson, Johnson and Iba (Photo courtesy of Herschel Nissenson)

⬤

In 1980, Oklahoma edged Colorado 82-42. How bad was it?

Johnson, then the coach at Oklahoma State, told me that when he watched the game film, a Colorado defender hardly ever appeared in the picture when Oklahoma ran the option pitch.

Late in the game, a Colorado manager knocked on the door of the Oklahoma coaches booth in the press box and said, "Coach [Chuck] Fairbanks says he hates to ask this, but could you possibly just run up the middle for a while?"

The Sooners obliged—and scored two touchdowns in about five minutes.

⬤

Let me say this in defense of Jimmy Johnson—he got an undeserved rap for allegedly rolling it up when Miami crushed Notre Dame 58-7 in Gerry Faust's last game as coach of the Irish in 1985.

First of all, Notre Dame came to Miami on Wednesday and was terribly prepared for the game, as unready to play as any team I've ever seen. Lou Holtz already had been named as Faust's successor, and there was no way the Irish could save Gerry's job.

When the score became 58-7 during the fourth quarter, I went down to the sidelines and told Johnson that

59 points was the single-game record for a Notre Dame opponent. Nevertheless, he called off the dogs, although Brent Musburger and Ara Parseghian, who were broadcasting the game for CBS-TV, convinced the world otherwise.

Paterno and the Polls

It came as something of a shock to me a few years ago when Joe Paterno's name showed up among the voters in the coaches' poll.

For years, Paterno refused to participate in the poll, although he always said he would be happy to cast a bal-

Joe Paterno (Penn State University)

lot at the end of the season. For years, the only poll that mattered to him was the Paterno Poll, a one-man operation run by you-know-who. This particular poll was taken in 1968, 1969 and 1973, when Penn State posted perfect seasons, yet didn't win any national championships; the results of the Paterno Poll were not entirely unexpected.

In a 1986 Associated Press story, Paterno expressed his feelings about the polls as follows:

"I don't think anybody in their right mind can be accurate during the season. If somebody would say to me the Sunday after a game, 'You rank the top 20 teams in the country,' it's a guessing game. I've got better things to do.

"If the fans are that interested in the weekly poll, I can't do anything about that. But that doesn't mean I've got to participate."

And in a press conference on October 17, 1989, Paterno said:

"I don't think polls do anything for anybody playing college football. I think they may do something for the fans, but not the players or the coaches. Some people may like to see themselves rated, but that has never been my cup of tea."

In a mid-1990s press conference, the subject of the polls came up again and Paterno made a crack about consulting his "advisor." That would be Budd Thalman, Penn State's associate athletic director for communications.

"Budd advises me, tells me what he thinks [about Paterno's ballot] and I say fine," Paterno said.

This is not an uncommon practice. The "coaches" poll has always been a misnomer; it should be the sports information directors' poll—or worse. When Jerry Claiborne was coaching, his wife usually filled out his ballot. Even former Nebraska coach Tom Osborne conceded recently that he didn't know much, if anything, about many of the teams on his ballot.

"I still think the polls are ridiculous," Paterno said. "But a couple of years ago, some fellow coaches told me I ought to vote because they were trying to get together with a trophy and I'm one of the older and more prominent coaches. Charlie Mac [McClendon, former executive director of the American Football Coaches Association] was trying to get more and more coaches active. He said, 'I know you don't believe in the polls, but . . .'"

To some, like cynical ol' me, this might smack of hypocrisy, which my dictionary defines as "pretending to be what one is not, or to feel what one does not feel." Paterno doesn't see it that way.

"I don't think it's hypocritical," he said. "Times change. It's no big deal. I don't have any problem about it, no problem where we're ranked. I'm not lobbying for anything. To me it's no big deal, not a very important thing, but I don't think it's hypocritical.

"I realize why the polls are there. If people pay that much attention to them and they create fan interest in college football, as long as I don't take them seriously . . ."

What helped sour Paterno on the polls, of course, were the voting in 1968, 1969 and 1973, years in which unbeaten-untied Penn State teams finished second (to

Ohio State), second (to Texas, which had help from President Richard Nixon and his infamous plaque) and fifth (behind 11-0 Notre Dame, 10-0-1 Ohio State, 10-0-1 Oklahoma and 11-1 Alabama). I don't see Penn State offering to give back the 1982 national championship because the 11-1 Lions, with a 42-21 loss to Alabama, finished ahead of an 11-0-1 SMU team.

At the time, it was the worst loss ever suffered by a team that went on to win the national championship. And that year's poll was a perfect example of why we need a playoff.

After holding down the No. 2 spot in the AP poll (behind Georgia) for three weeks, SMU played ninth-ranked Arkansas, 8-1 at the time.

The Mustangs, playing their final regular-season game, trailed 17-10, but scored with about five minutes remaining. A tie assured them of the Southwest Conference championship and a berth in the Cotton Bowl; a loss, and Texas, with two games remaining, could have beaten them out.

So SMU kicked the point and it may have cost the Mustangs the national championship. Had they gone for two and made it, who knows how the vote would have come out? As it was, the tie dropped SMU to fourth place.

A playoff is something that Paterno, a liberal Republican, and I, an ultra-conservative Conservative, agree on. After all, we both claimed Brooklyn as our home for quite a few years.

"I have been for a playoff because I felt we had some teams, in 1968-69 especially, that were as good as any in the country and never got voted national champions or had a shot at the championship," Paterno said around the time he gave in and became a voter. "I have always kind of resented the fact that they say we have had two national championships (1982 and 1986). I like to think we had five. I think the '68, '69 and '73 teams were national champions. They won all of their games and beat good bowl teams."

Years ago, Paterno used to say that if he were in an accident and needed a brain transplant, he would want the brain of an athletic director because it had never been used. When Joe became an athletic director, he changed it to the brain of a sports writer.

He must have loved that commercial where a dumpy looking sports writer used a dartboard to pick the national champion and his dart landed on fictitious 0-11 Boise Tech. We may have disagreed on Paterno's participation in the coaches' poll, but we're both for a playoff. And you can have what's left of my brain any time.

Penn State and the New York writers had it out on a couple of earlier occasions.

In 1971, Penn State was pushing tailback Lydell Mitchell for the Heisman Trophy. His chief competition came from Auburn quarterback Pat Sullivan, the eventual winner, and Cornell tailback Ed Marinaro.

In those days, Penn State included with its weekly release a newsletter written by the late Ridge Riley, who was head of Penn State's alumni association and a fellow who bled blue and white.

Nissenson and Paterno with trophy (Photo courtesy of Herschel Nissenson)

Week after week Riley would castigate Marinaro more than he plugged Mitchell. His argument was, "How can anyone vote for an Ivy Leaguer over a great star from Penn State, where they play real football?"

Both Gordon White of the *New York Times* and I told Penn State it was its job to promote Mitchell as best it could, but to stop knocking Marinaro because he played for an Ivy League school. Remember, Marinaro was college football's rushing king at the time.

The next skirmish with Penn State came in 1977. I had mentioned in passing in a late-season story on possible bowl pairings that Pittsburgh had crushed Temple 76-0, while Penn State beat the Owls 44-7. John Morris, then Penn State's sports information director, was on the phone almost as soon as the story hit the wire to point out that the exalted and compassionate St. Joe Paterno had lifted his starters midway through the first period— or some such nonsense—while Pitt intentionally rolled it up.

The you-know-what really hit the fan on November 21 at the weekly New York writers' luncheon. The Orange Bowl had chosen sixth-ranked Arkansas over No. 9 Penn State and No. 10 Pittsburgh as the opponent for Oklahoma, whose coach, Barry Switzer, was an Arkansas grad, and the good burghers of State College, Pennsylvania, didn't like it. The Orange Bowl always had the repu-

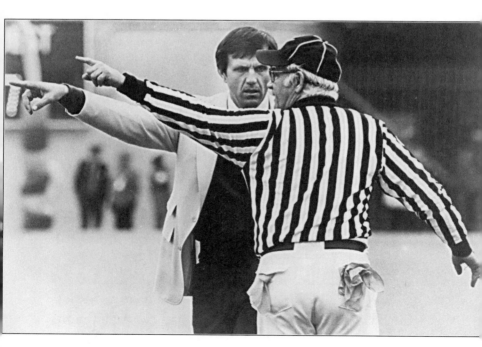

Jackie Sherrill (University of Pittsburgh)

tation of choosing the highest-ranked team available and simply followed its long-standing practice.

We had both Pitt coach Jackie Sherrill and Paterno on a phone hookup at our luncheon. Sherrill said something to the effect that the selection of Arkansas was a slap in the face of Eastern football. As emcee of the luncheon, I asked Paterno if he agreed with Sherrill.

"That's for you guys to decide because a lot of the blame can be vested on you people up there," he answered.

"Are you blaming someone up here for your not going to the Orange Bowl?" I asked.

Said Paterno: "A lot of people like you are enamored of other parts of the country.

Added John Morris, "The Orange Bowl became convinced that Penn State was going to lose to Pitt [they didn't]." Morris told me, "They read your stuff . . . you have no idea how much faith bowl committees put in your stuff."

Hogwash!

69

The Media

Don't believe everything you read in the paper. I know you've heard that line before. Let me go one better —take it with a large grain of salt if it comes from the AP wire.

I have been a member of the media for near on half a century, but I have never gone around defending the media because I'm not a big fan of certain aspects of the profession.

The best description of modern-day journalism I ever heard was told to me by Tom Osborne, the former Nebraska coach, roughly two decades ago. Said Dr. Tom: "What journalism has become is—bad news is good news and good news is no news."

Truer words were never spoken.

Take general columnists, for example. You make someone a general columnist and he or she automatically becomes an expert on everything under the sun.

I can write a decent column on college football or major league baseball because I have covered those sports extensively. But I would never attempt a column on horse racing or boxing because I don't know enough about them.

Coaches can rarely escape the media.

I was flying to a coaches' golf tournament one year when it was obvious that Doug Dickey was in trouble at the University of Florida. The Florida media had been on his case something fierce.

There in the seat directly in front of me was Doug Dickey.

"Doug," I said, "you may have gotten away from the Florida media, but here's the national media breathing down your neck."

One year I was flying to Houston en route to College Station. I was wearing an Oklahoma State golf shirt, with the letters OSU on the breast pocket.

"Oh," breathed one of the flight attendants, "I went to Ohio State, too."

"Sorry," I said. "This is the real OSU—Oklahoma State.

"By the way," I added, "what do they think of my friend John Cooper in Columbus?"

"That goddamn John Cooper," she snorted. "He can't beat Michigan. We'd rather play against him than for him."

That same flight was 45 minutes late leaving New York, and I had a 45-minute layover to catch a flight from Houston to College Station.

When I asked the flight attendant to have the captain radio ahead and possibly hold the connecting flight for a few minutes, she said, "Why are you going to College Station?"

"To cover a football game," I said.

"Oh, yes," she breathed, "that's the team with the extra man [Texas A&M's 12th man]."

One of the rules in the Philadelphia bureau during the World War II days was that the sports wire had to carry the score of the Slippery Rock football game. Believe it or not, it was used as a tie-breaker in a lot of office pools.

One Saturday the score was late in arriving and Pennsylvania members were getting antsy, even though the school is located in Pennsylvania. Ted Meier had messaged New York several times looking for the score.

Suddenly a radio station called about a rumor that Hitler was dead. Meier decided to kill two birds with one message. He sent the following classic to New York:

"Radio member hears Hitler dead.

"How pls Slippery Rock?"

If I ever write a book about the AP, that will be the title—"How Please Slippery Rock?"

ESPN likes to bill itself as "The Worldwide Leader in Sports." Sometimes I had to wonder during the five football seasons I worked there.

The year 1992 marked the 10th anniversary of Bear Bryant's last game. During a GameDay production meeting—television networks have more production meetings than dogs have fleas—I suggested that the 10th anniversary of Bryant's swan song, followed by his death a month later, should be addressed on the air.

The producer, whose name I don't recall, said, "Sell me on it."

I said—to myself—"If I have to sell you on Bear Bryant, you shouldn't be handling college football."

Every decent-size town has a stringer who sticks his microphone into everyone's face and sells his tape to whoever will pay a few bucks for it.

The one in Nashville is a roly-poly little fellow named Sherman Something-Or-Other.

When Florida visited Vanderbilt in 1996, Florida coach Steve Spurrier agreed to meet the press in a room Vandy had set up, which would have meant coming back outside and across the field.

But Spurrier changed his mind when fans threw stuff at him as he left the field and decided to face the media right outside the Gators' dressing room.

Sherman was the last one to hear of the change in plans. By the time he reached Spurrier, the coach was surrounded and Sherman couldn't poke his microphone through the crowd and Spurrier wasn't about to do a second interview session.

Sherman looked around and saw a Florida player sitting by a table in the end zone with only a handful of writers talking to him.

Sherman stuck his mike in the player's face and asked, "Your performance today?"

The player politely assessed his performance.

The next question was, "Did Vanderbilt do anything to surprise you?"

"Not really. We knew they had a good defense. They played us tough last year, they had great schemes and we just had to hang in there and get what we could get. If we're fortunate we can learn something from this game, blah-blah-blah."

Sherm's last question: "Your name and position?"

The Florida writers were splitting their sides from laughing so hard.

The player looked at Sherman and replied, "I'm Danny Wuerffel; I play quarterback."

I forget the game—I think it was a Fiesta Bowl—in which UCLA was one of the teams.

UCLA intercepted a pass, but I could see at one end of the TV screen that a penalty flag had been thrown.

The coaches were miked and color analyst John Brodie said, "Let's go down and hear UCLA's first play from Terry Donahue."

I remember thinking, maybe they should wait to see what the penalty was. Sure enough, the penalty over-turned UCLA's interception.

Nevertheless, the network switched to Donahue, who said, "Oh, shit!"

Brodie never lost his aplomb. "That must be some first play," he quipped.

A former editor once told me that lacerations, abrasions and contusions should appear in print as cuts, scrapes and bruises for readers who aren't used to multi-syllabic words. Also, that no one "reveals" anything because revelations can only come from on high. An earthly being can disclose, but only God can reveal.

In 1979, Rutgers visited Knoxville and upset Tennessee 13-7.

A Knoxville writer named Ben Byrd wrote a tongue-in-cheek advance column wanting to know, "What are rutgers? Are they like yonkers? Can you buy just one rutger?"

Tongue-in-cheek became foot-in-mouth after Rutgers upset Tennessee. Ben Byrd was later awarded an honorary varsity 'R.'

Woody and "Little Woody"

I didn't have many dealings with Woody Hayes. One was more than enough.

In 1970, I was president of the Football Writers Association of New York. We held a luncheon every Monday during the season. ABC paid for a telephone hookup and we tried to get at least one coach from an upcoming TV game on the horn. I arranged these calls a week or so in advance.

Woody Hayes (SPI Archives)

I had never met or talked to Woody Hayes. And I was told it was impossible to get hold of him during the season.

The Ohio State-Michigan game was scheduled for Nov. 21 on ABC. On November 8, I called Hayes' home (his number was always listed in the Columbus phone book). I explained to Mrs. Hayes, a lovely person, why I needed to speak with Woody. She gave me a number and said, "If he's near any phone, this is the one."

I dialed the number. A man answered.

"Coach Hayes, please," I said.

"This is Coach Hayes," the voice said.

I couldn't believe my luck, which would run out a week later. I explained that we wanted to have him on a phone hookup on Monday, November 16. Woody was gracious. He said he had his own luncheon on Mondays, but told me to call around 1:15 and if he wasn't there to try again a few minutes later.

Sure enough, that's what happened. On my second try, Woody was there as promised.

In 1969, Bo Schembechler's first year as head coach at Michigan, the Wolverines upset Woody and Ohio State 24-12, spoiling the Buckeyes' perfect season and denying them a shot at the national championship. Woody was so infuriated that he refused to say the word "Michigan" and had his players wipe their feet on Michigan doormats just outside the locker room the following season.

Since it was late in the season and I was in charge of the AP All-America team and Ohio State had another great team, I wanted to know which Buckeyes should be considered as potential All-Americans without coming right out and asking the question in those words.

I had seen a quote attributed to Woody that "you can't have a great team unless your seniors are playing up to their capabilities." He agreed he had said that.

"Can you tell us which of your seniors are playing the best?" I asked.

"I won't answer any questions about any of my players," he answered.

I was slightly miffed. I turned the question around.

"Well, can you tell us which of your seniors are not playing up to your capabilities?" I tried.

"I just told you I won't answer any questions about any of my players," he snapped, "and if you were a legitimate writer you wouldn't ask me that question."

I thanked Woody for his time and hung up.

Lou Holtz was on Woody Hayes' staff in 1968 as secondary coach.

"We beat Michigan 50-14 in the last game of the regular season and after our last touchdown we scored on a two-point conversion," Holtz remembers. "After the game they asked Coach Hayes why he went for two and he said, 'Because they wouldn't let me go for three.'"

●

The Rose Bowl of January 1, 1969, between USC and Ohio State was the final game of O.J. Simpson's college career. In the second quarter, Simpson ran 80 yards for a touchdown. Hayes grabbed assistant coach Holtz and demanded, "Why did O.J. go 80 yards?"

Holtz claims he replied, "That's all he needed, Coach."

If Holtz really said that, he's probably lucky he lived to tell about it.

●

In late December of 1978 I was in New Orleans to cover the Alabama-Penn State Sugar Bowl. The plan was for me to fly up to Jacksonville for the Ohio State-Clemson Gator Bowl on December 29 and then return to New Orleans.

However, a few days before the Gator Bowl, AP sports editor Wick Temple told me, "Forget about the Gator Bowl. It's not that important. Just stay in New Orleans."

I was crushed. Who wouldn't jump at the chance to go from New Orleans to Jacksonville? Just kidding.

The Hilton Hotel in New Orleans was headquarters for the Southeastern Conference. I watched the Gator Bowl in the SEC's hospitality suite with a number of people, including Tennessee coach Johnny Majors and Kentucky coach Fran Curci.

It turned out to be Woody Hayes' last game because he slugged Clemson nose guard Charlie Bauman, who had intercepted a late pass and gone out of bounds on the Ohio State sideline.

It happened so quickly none of us was really sure what had transpired.

"Did he punch him?" Curci asked.

"They ought to fire the son of a bitch," Majors said.

Ohio State did, and the next day I had to get comment.

"This is a sad way to end a glorious career," Majors began

"Whoa," I said. "What happened to 'They ought to fire the son of a bitch?'"

Because he played for Woody Hayes at Miami of Ohio and later coached under him at Ohio State, Bo Schembechler became known as "Little Woody" when he assumed the head coaching job at Michigan in 1969.

The epithet was undeserved. Oh, Bo could growl and throw temper tantrums like Woody, but he was basically a good guy. You could needle Bo back and he could take it as well as dish it out.

In the 1970s, the American Football Coaches Association had a tie-in with the Tea Council of the U.S.A. Every spring, a different head coach would come to New York and we'd visit for a spell.

Bo was the visiting coach one year and we went for a drink (something other than tea, as I recall) at the Top of the Sixes, an establishment atop a sky-

Bo Schembechler (University of Michigan)

scraper at 666 Fifth Avenue. It was the year after Michigan lost four games directly attributable to breakdowns in the kicking game.

As we sat down, Bo looked at me and needled, "You now, you write some of the most horseshit stories I've ever read."

"That may be," I replied, "but I've never had a story blocked."

Bo's 1984 Michigan team, which had a mediocre 6-5 record, played 11-0 and top-ranked Brigham Young in the Holiday Bowl. It rained in San Diego much of that late-December week and it was actually colder there than in Buffalo, N.Y. The *San Diego Union* ran a box on the front page every day to prove it.

Bo and the Wolverines arrived on a wet Tuesday for a Friday night game. Bo was an hour or so late to a press conference, and when he arrived, BYU coach LaVell Edwards said, "Welcome to San Diego."

"Aaarrrggghhh," Bo growled, "it's your home game, isn't it (the Western Athletic Conference champion was the host team)? How come every time we go to a bowl we're always the visiting team? (the Pac-10 team was always considered the host team in the Rose Bowl)."

This was one of the two years there was such a thing as the Cherry Bowl in the Pontiac (Michigan) Silverdome. Poker-faced, Edwards inquired of Bo, "Isn't there a bowl in Detroit you could have gone to?"

That shut Bo up until someone asked how he could justify bringing a 6-5 team to play the No. 1-ranked team in the nation.

Bo harked back to the stretch between 1972-74 when Michigan never went to a bowl despite a 30-2-1 record and a couple of Big Ten championships. Because of the Big Ten's no-repeat rule, a ban on participation in all other bowls and one year a vote by conference athletic directors in favor of Ohio State, the Wolverines were shut out of post-season action. Bo allowed as how the Holiday Bowl made up for some of that.

Knowing Bo as well as I did, I could get away with what I did next.

I went up to him and said, "You're lucky you didn't go to a bowl game in those three years."

He bit. "Why?" he asked.

"Because," I said, "your bowl record would be 2-12 instead of 2-9."

Bo muttered something which I didn't stick around long enough to hear.

If Fielding H. Yost wasn't invited to many West Virginia homecomings, it was perfectly understandable. First of all, Yost served as Michigan's head coach from 1901 to 23 and 1925-26 and was athletic director from 1921 to 1941, so he was usually occupied on autumn Saturdays.

However, Yost (West Virginia '95) may have been persona non grata at his alma mater. The two schools have met only once, in 1904. Michigan and Yost came away 130-0 winners.

Bumper Sticker—
"Give 'Em Hell, Pell"

I was there when my best friend tried to kill himself.

On February 2, 1994, I was in Charley Pell's house in Jacksonville, Florida, chatting with his wife, Ward, waiting for Charley to come home. Instead, we received the news of his suicide attempt. I have had nicer welcomes.

Charley Pell *(University of Florida)*

However, in less than a year's time, Charley Pell not only had done a complete turnaround with his life, but was back on the sidelines coaching in the Hula Bowl.

Since the Hula Bowl was an ESPN production, the rival head coaches were Mike Gottfried and Lee Corso. Each was permitted to invite two former coaches to assist him. Corso chose Don James and Pepper Rodgers; Gottfried took Rey Dempsey and Pell. I had suggested Pell's name to Gottfried several weeks earlier and Mike took it from there. The real tragedy is that Pell was never able to get back into coaching for real.

The trip back from "total darkness," as Pell described his 1994 depression, was slow but steady. Several weeks at a depression clinic in Georgia started Charley on the way back.

In February 1994, my plans were to visit the Pells for a few days en route to a banquet in Orlando honoring Charlie McClendon, who was retiring as executive director of the American Football Coaches Association.

I arrived at the Pells' around 5 o'clock. Around 5:30, Linda Jowers came over to say hello—or so we thought. Linda and her husband, Malcolm (CQ), then a lieutenant in the Florida Highway Patrol, lived close by. Malcom has been in charge of security for the University of Florida's football coaches since Pell's days—he's the uniformed trooper you now see behind Steve Spurrier—and they have remained close friends and golfing buddies.

What we didn't know was that Malcolm had received Charley's suicide note, including a map and detailed instructions where to find the body—in his car in a wooded area a few miles away—and sent Linda to be with Ward when the news came.

Bad as it was, the news was good. Charley was alive.

Fortunately, Charley Pell, perhaps the most organized coach I have ever known, was running behind schedule that day. To speed up the process, he took some sleeping pills and drank a bottle of vodka before running a hose from the car's exhaust pipe into the car. The combination made him so sick that he got out of the car to throw up. That's when they found him.

If Charley Pell is organized, he is also somewhat absentminded. Many coaches have one-track minds. When he coached at Florida, he once registered to vote in a different district than his wife because he couldn't remember his address.

We can joke some about it now, and some of Pell's friends have decided that Charley probably survived because he took some No-Doz pills, drank a six-pack of nonalcoholic brew and forgot to gas up the car.

Around 6:15, Malcom Jowers called Linda, who informed Ward and me. We went to the hospital, where Charley was in a state of grogginess and mumbling incoherently.

Much of the next two days was spent in Charley's hospital room, a VIP room where he was listed under a fictitious name so the hospital could honestly say they had no Charley Pell registered.

You can't keep something like this under wraps though. Sure enough, the next morning a caller to a radio talk show reported that "my girlfriend works at Baptist Hospital and she says they brought Charley Pell in last night after he tried to kill himself." Little by little the story got out.

It was almost two days before Charley was able to talk coherently and move around. I have rarely been at a loss for words, but what do you say at a time like that? Charley wouldn't see anyone, and when a former player drove up from Gainesville, Charley sent word downstairs to "tell him I love him, but I don't want to see anyone right now." He was doing some deep thinking; you could almost hear the wheels turning in his head.

Before leaving for Orlando, I had to say something.

"You know," I said, "if Coach Bryant (Charley played for the Bear at Alabama) were alive, he'd come down here and kick your butt."

"Yeah," Charley said, "I almost got to tell him myself."

"That," I replied, "is assuming you would have wound up in the same place."

Charley is thinking straight once again after going through what his psychiatrist called "the most real part" of his life. I have never asked Charley why he did what he did, and I never intend to, but I have never known him to do anything without what he perceived to be a good reason. When we finally got around to some serious talk, Charley explained, or tried to, that "53 years of history can not be put on the table. You could write a psychology book with that answer."

Suffice to say that if you've never been where Pell was, you can't understand it. I haven't, and I don't. I only know it takes more guts than I have to try something like that.

"Can I put it into words? I doubt it," Charley told me. "If I could, I could put it in book form. In my mind, and in the minds of people who have been in darkness, you don't have to explain it, total darkness being figuratively hopelessness; that's the darkness—hopelessness.

"We're speaking what's in my mind, trying to describe something for you to see, which is awfully hard to do. I remember the expressions and the words that came out of my wife's mouth when she came out of childbirth. She said, 'Charley, I never knew there could have been so much pain.' I said, 'Well, I understand how you feel.' At that moment, if looks would have killed, I wouldn't be here today. The reason was I had no way to understand. To be in the bottom of the hole is total darkness. That's hopelessness."

Ward Pell is the perfect coach's wife. She knows how to entertain and she's a great storyteller, especially where it concerns Charley. Give a listen:

"Shortly after moving to Gainesville, we had moved from the Hilton into the Holiday Inn because the Holiday Inn was closer to the university and it was evident that our house was not going to be ready for quite a while. We were able to secure an old home that the university had owned that was about a block from the Holiday Inn.

"It had been quite a showplace in 1924, but by 1979 it was a holy disaster. It had a beautiful yard, but we lived inside the house.

"At that time, we were probably spending more time going to the airport and creating the Gator Club concept, so Charley really didn't come home very much.

"This one particular night we had an actual social event there in town, and a good friend of ours had a daughter who was a senior in high school, and she said she would baby-sit for our son, who was 10 at the time.

"After we got home, Charley needed to take Kelly home. In the process of going to her home, he was pulled over by one of Gainesville's finest. The policeman asked him for his driver's license and of course his driver's license said Clemson, South Carolina. We had just moved.

"The officer asked him, 'Coach, do you know what your address here in Gainesville is?'

"And he looked over at Kelly and he said, 'Kelly, what's the name of that street I live on? I know it's the [Addison] Pound House and it's down that way, but I don't know the street.' So Kelly had to bail him out of that one.

"We finally got in our real home when it was completed in September. By this time everybody had their legal driver's license for the State of Florida; we were real citizens.

"We had to register to vote. I told him where the place was to go and vote and we had a good friend running for the Senate and we were gonna make sure that he got elected. Charley went to vote and he went to the wrong poll.

"The lady says, 'Coach Pell, you don't live in this district.' He said, 'Well, I live just right up there,' which was not far from this poll, but unfortunately it was not our poll. They let him go ahead and vote. I don't know whether that was legal or not.

"Then we were going to Mexico and we land coming back and we were going through customs and I was telling them where I lived—2405 NW 23rd Terrace, Gainesville, Florida. Charley walks up right behind me; it's very evident we're man and wife traveling together. And the guy asks him where he lived and he said he lived at 2504 NW 24th Terrace. He had no clue that was not his address. I think it was [basketball coach[Norm Sloan's address.

"The guy said, 'You married?' I said, 'Yes, we have a rather large house. Actually, he doesn't know where he lives, so it's okay.'"

Sportswriters aren't always smarter than coaches.

The night before the Alabama-Florida game in 1979, I was sitting with Charley Pell by the pool at the Holiday Inn in Ocala, where the Florida team bunked on Friday night.

"Who's the best offensive coordinator in the country?" Pell asked.

I said Galen Hall. He hired Mike Shanahan. The rest is history.

Galen Hall (University of Florida)

What Hath God Wrought

You may have heard of the AP college football poll. I handled it for two decades with my pocket calculator.

I didn't have a vote; no AP staffer did. But that didn't stop college football fanatics from sending missives—no missiles, thank goodness—that usually began, "How could you . . . "

The business of ranking teams actually began in 1926, a decade before the AP got into the act. University of Illinois Prof. Frank Dickinson admitted to one of his classes one day that he liked to rank college football teams using a mathematical formula.

One of his students was the sports editor of the *Daily Illini* and wrote a story about the prof's unusual hobby. A Chicago clothing manufacturer named Jack Rissman saw the story and approached Dickinson about using his formula to rank the teams in the Big Nine—it didn't become the Big Ten until later—since all of the teams in the conference did not play each other (and still don't).

The Dickinson Big Nine rankings were of interest to Notre Dame coach Knute Rockne. One college football researcher says Rockne contacted Dickinson about using his formula to rate the best teams in the country.

According to said researcher:

"Rockne said to him, 'You know, I had a pretty good team back in 1924. I want you to go back over 1924 and 1925 and do your system on those seasons, just to see if I'd be No. 1.'

"So he did two retroactive seasons. And sure enough, the '24 Notre Dame team ended up in first. That, in a nutshell, was the Dickinson system."

From 1926 through 1940, Dickinson's top-ranked team at the end of each season received a trophy as the nation's mythical champion. The trophy was retired in 1940 after Minnesota won it for a third time.

Two things took place in 1935. I turned a year old and AP sports editor Alan J. Gould came out with his personal postseason rankings. In an amazing example of fence-straddling, Gould, who received input from friends and colleagues, named 8-0 Minnesota, 9-0 Princeton and 12-0 SMU as tri-champions for the 1935 season.

Riots would break out if that happened today and there might even be a congressional investigation. Back then, Gould was merely hanged in effigy in one Minnesota town, which didn't like the idea of having to share the "national championship."

"It was a case of thinking up ideas to develop interest and controversy," Gould said. "Papers wanted material to fill space between games. That's all I had in mind, something to keep the pot boiling. Sports then was living off controversy (What else is new?), opinion, whatever. This was just another exercise in hoopla."

Although Gould is credited with originating the AP poll, the idea came from Cy Sherman of the *Lincoln* (Nebraska) *Star*, who suggested that Gould poll sports editors of AP-affiliated newspapers in 1936. He did. The first AP poll was taken on October 19, 1936 (The preseason poll didn't begin until 1950), and there were seven polls during the regular season (the postbowl poll had a one-year tryout in 1965 and was adopted permanently in 1968; UPI didn't go that route until 1975, after its national champions lost bowl games in 1965 (Michigan State), 1970 (Texas) and 1973 (Alabama).

Minnesota was ranked No. 1 (35 voters participated in the inaugural poll) in the first two polls and the last two, with Northwestern holding down the top spot in the middle three. Minnesota was ranked No. 1 at the end of the season, even though the Wolverines lost to Northwestern 6-0 on October 31, a game that started Northwestern's three-week stay at the top of the rankings (Northwestern has been ranked No. 1 only twice since, both times in mid-1962.)

Both Minnesota and Northwestern finished 7-1 that year. However, Northwestern lost its final game, 26-0 to Notre Dame, and slipped all the way to No. 7. So in that very first year a rule of thumb was born—if you're going to lose a game, lose it early.

The AP poll soon became the standard by which college football teams were judged. Dickinson junked his rankings after the 1940 season, and the AP didn't have much opposition until United Press kicked off a poll of its own in 1950 using coaches as the voters. In 1958, United Press merged with International News Service and became UPI, which has since lost (1) numerous members over the years, and (2) the coaches poll to *USA Today*/CNN and now *USA Today*/ESPN.

For a time, any sports writer who worked for an AP member could vote. The final poll in 1954, for example, attracted 409 ballots. The first year of panel voting was 1960, and there are currently 70 voters, apportioned geographically depending on how many Division I-A teams each state has. The basic, but not mathematically exact, formula is one-half vote for each Division I-A team. The votes are counted on a 25-24-23-22-21, etc., basis, down to one point for No. 25.

The poll used to be the Top Twenty, which had a nice ring to it. An AP sports editor named Darrell Christian, whose main claim to fame was drinking, changed it to the Top 25. Since teams that didn't make the Top Twenty were listed as "others receiving votes," with their point totals, any imbecile could have deciphered which team was No. 21, No. 22, etc.

In 1999, Florida State became the first team to be ranked No. 1 in every poll from the preseason to the postseason (When voting was based only on the regular season, Notre Dame in 1943 and Army in 1945 were No. 1 each week).

Perhaps the most memorable poll was the last regular-season one in 1979.

After holding down the No. 1 spot for seven straight weeks, Alabama (11-0) struggled past Auburn 25-18 in an unimpressive performance and slipped to No. 2, behind Ohio State (11-0), which had completed its regular season a week earlier by defeating Michigan 18-15.

We usually had to chase down several voters each week for their ballots. When we saw how close the vote was going to be, we started the chase early. And we held the poll most of the day—well past the scheduled release time—until we had all but one ballot. As I recall, it was a voter from Colorado who had covered a Colorado State game in Hawaii and stayed there on vacation. Even his paper couldn't find him.

We finally went without his ballot and Ohio State sneaked ahead of Alabama by 1 1/2 points, even though Bama had more first-place votes (29) than the Buckeyes (16). So did No. 3 Southern California (19). What happened was that eight voters failed to rank Alabama among the top three.

By the way, when we finally tracked down the missing voter, it turned out his ballot wouldn't have affected the rankings.

That didn't matter to Alabamians. It's a miracle the mailman didn't get a hernia from lugging all the letters from Alabama. It didn't help when a Birmingham sportscaster flashed my name and the AP's address across the screen and suggested that a complaint or two might be nice. It turned out to be one or two hundred.

The nicer ones started out "Dear Scrooge" and "To What Big Dummy It May Concern" and ended "Hatefully."

The first missive to arrive was a telegram from a lady (I think because her name was Sheila) in Sycamore, Alabama. It began, "I think the AP poll sucks" and went on to refer to "your eight chicken-shit voters."

Here are some excerpts from other correspondence— "I do not think that you are a very nice person . . . You should not even be allowed to sit on the AP pole [sic] . . . Even Santa Claus should be mad at you (Remember, this was December) . . . I hope on Christmas Eve that you have nightmares and all you can see is Roll Tide."

—"For eight voters to omit Alabama from their top three choices is absolutely a horrendous act . . . It is obvious that you overlooked it altogether because you are probably part of the campaign to draft USC for national champions."

—"Well, you've done it again, haven't you? I think it's a shame that the money-grubbing bowl politicians are able to control who gets No. 1 at the end of the year."

—"How can a team that has been voted No. 1 for seven straight weeks fall in the rankings when they win their final game, then take a team that is idle and ranked No. 2 and replace the top team? It sounds like a set-up by the sports writers to have the Rose Bowl for the national championship."

—"I know that you can't tell the people how to vote, but you damn sure can see that more responsible people are appointed as voters next time."

—"Alabama proved their championship qualities in coming from behind in the fourth quarter, driving 82 yards to beat an 8-3 Auburn team. However, Ohio State had to block a punt to beat an 8-3 Michigan team. I sincerely hope this will be under serious consideration after the bowl games are completed."

—"How can eight voters leave them out of the top three and still look at themselves in the mirror? It's pure, simple politics, as usual."

—"It is my opinion that people are against the South and I disagree on how Alabama has dropped from No. 1 and don't understand and I would like a return letter if you could enlighten me on the subject because this is football country and if you could have been one of the 80,000 people to attend the Alabama-Auburn game you would agree completely."

—"Whoever voted Ohio State No. 1 is not being fair and is not in their right mind."

—"My husband and I think that it is stupid and sad that the AP poll doesn't know its job well enough to know that Alabama is and always will be No. 1."

—"You people say Alabama played a weak schedule. Yeah, they might have, but they beat every damnbody they played, you silly damn Yankee."

—"What do you mean placing the great Tide No. 2?"

—"I think your point of voting is about as sicking [sic] as Komenie [sic]."

(Ed. Note: Be that as it may, I once had an Alabamian tell me during the hostage crisis, "Ah'd vote for Eyeran before ah'd vote for Notre Dame.")

—"Alabama will be the No. 1 team in the nation regardless of your eight idiots."

—"My suggestion to you is for you to get a few more competent people to do your voting and hopefully they will also possess enough fortitude to place football teams in an order that won't show such obvious partiality toward Southern football (say what?)."

—"After seeing and hearing the results of the AP poll, I am completely disgusted, although I expected as much. What does AP really stand for—Always Prejudiced? And to think that the majority of Americans think that the South discriminates."

—"Well, it looks like our Crimson Tide has been shot down for the third year in a row."

—"You must have some kind of odd reporters. You did it to Alabama last year."

(Alabamians conveniently forgot that the Crimson Tide won the 1978 AP national championship despite losing to USC 24-14 in Birmingham, a game I covered and which wasn't as close as the score would indicate.)

There also was a letter from Hoover, Alabama, to wit:

"Once again the AP has goofed. I fail to understand how Baylor, 7-4, can be ranked in the Top Twenty and other quality 7-4 teams such as Tennessee and Notre Dame unranked."

Not even so much as a Roll Tide.

All worked out well for Alabama, though. The Tide defeated Arkansas 24-9 in the Sugar Bowl and won the national championship when USC edged Ohio State 17-16 in the Rose Bowl, just as Bear Bryant ordered.

All worked out well for me, too. I sold a magazine piece based on all those letters.

The final 1966 poll also is a sore point in Alabama. That was the year Notre Dame and Michigan played their infamous 10-10 tie in late November and finished 1-2 with identical 9-0-1 records ahead of an 11-0 Alabama outfit which Bryant always said (privately) was his best team ever.

Bryant always held a news conference on Wednesday before an Alabama game. In 1978, Bama was No. 1 in the preseason poll, and an Alabama writer—one of the many who referred to the Crimson Tide as "we"—asked Bryant how he thought "we'd do" and how he liked being No. 1 to start the season.

"Well," the Bear drawled, looking at me, "I remember in 1966 we started out No. 1, won 'em all and finished third."

I don't think Bryant ever really believed that I had nothing to do with the poll until a few years later.

Every year in its media guide, Michigan lists its 1947 team as "national champs." Not so.

Because coaches and writers don't always see eye-to-eye, college football has had two national champions a number of times. Not many people remember this, but there was one year when the writers couldn't even agree among themselves.

That year was 1947, when the AP took an unofficial postbowl poll AFTER voting Notre Dame the national championship . . . and the Irish didn't win that one, which has become known around Michigan as the Recount After the Roses.

When Notre Dame beat Southern Cal 38-7 in the 1947 regular-season finale—school policy prevented the Irish from going to a bowl between 1924 and 1969—it closed out a 9-0-0 season. But Michigan's 21-0 victory over Ohio State that gave the Wolverines a 9-0-0 regular-season record was not the end of their season. They still had to play Southern Cal, of all people, in the Rose Bowl.

Notre Dame and Michigan had flip-flopped between No. 1 and No. 2 all season in the AP rankings, which had it Notre Dame-Michigan in seven of the 10 polls—including the last one, the one that counted—and Michigan-Notre Dame in the other three.

Michigan went into its game with Ohio State ranked No. 1. But Notre Dame took over first place with a 59-6 rout of mighty Tulane, which won only two games all season, was shut out three times and scored seven points or less in three other games. Ohio State also won only two games that year, was blanked four times and twice was limited to one touchdown.

According to Will Perry's book *The Wolverines*, Coach Fritz Crisler warned his players, who were two-touchdown favorites in the Rose Bowl, "You are going out to California to play a football game."

Nevertheless, a good time was had by all. The Wolverines attended a rehearsal with Bob Hope, they met Edgar Bergen, Loretta Young and Marlene Dietrich, they toured the movie studios. All-American Bump Elliott and his brother, Pete, who earned four letters in golf, teed it up with Bing Crosby (Der Bingle won).

Before a crowd of 93,000 on New Year's Day, there was no doubt the Wolverines had come to play football. They buried USC 49-0, the third common opponent with Notre Dame. They also played Pitt (Notre Dame 40-6, Michigan 69-0) and Northwestern (Notre Dame

26-19, Michigan 49-21). Combined common-opponent scores: Notre Dame 104-32, Michigan 167-21.

In the next-to-last AP poll, Notre Dame had received 58 1/2 first-place votes and 1,184 points to Michigan's 541/2 and 1,176. But a controversy broke out after the final poll, which turned out to be no contest, with Notre Dame receiving 107 first-place votes and 1,410 points to Michigan's 25/1,289. First-place votes also went to 9-0-0 Penn State (1), 8-2-0 Alabama (1), 8-2-0 North Carolina (7) and 7-2-1 Oklahoma (1).

Sports writers demanded a new vote after the Rose Bowl. Were the Fighting Irish of Heisman Trophy winner Johnny Lujack, George Connor, Leon Hart and Ziggy Czarobski really better than the Wolverines of the Elliott brothers, Bob Chappuis and Al Wistert?

In a special two-team AP poll, an expanded list of 357 sports editors and football writers from coast-to-coast voted for Michigan by 226-119, with 12 calling it a draw. Some 54 voters had seen both teams play, and that bunch had it 33-17-4, also in favor of Michigan.

Even then, the voting wasn't over. In what probably was the first-ever UP poll, United Press polled 22 Southern Cal players, and 17 of them rated Notre Dame the better team.

A UP story of January 7, 1948, read: "The boys who took the beatings, Southern California's battered football squad, today picked Notre Dame over Michigan as the best team in the land.

"Regardless of polls by sports writers, a representative cross-section of the Trojan team chose the Irish as tops in their book."

The USC players asked to remain anonymous, but UP reported that one of them said, "We played a better game against Notre Dame than we did against Michigan, but with the Irish we just felt they had all the power in the world. We almost knew they were going to push right over us. Michigan pushed right over us, too, but it wasn't the same thing."

And minutes after the Rose Bowl pounding, USC coach Jeff Cravath had said, "Michigan wouldn't beat Notre Dame's first team."

So it is that you will find Notre Dame listed as the kings of college football for 1947 everywhere but in Michigan's annual media guide, where the 10-0-0 record for that year always carries the notation, "National Champs."

Actually Michigan was voted No. 1 in such polls as Berryman, Billingsley, Board, DeVold, Dunkel, Football Research, Houlgate, Litkenhous, National Championship Foundation and Poling. The Helms Foundation split its vote between Michigan and Notre Dame. Williamson and the AP, the most recognizable poll, went for Notre Dame.

The Boston Baked Bean

Carroll "Beano" Cook knows more about college football than I do, which is quite an admission for me to make.

Beano stories are legendary:

—When he was sports information director at the University of Pittsburgh, he went on the air in Lincoln, Nebraska, in 1958 and promised that Pitt coach John Michelosen was a compassionate sort and would not roll it up on the Cornhuskers. True to Beano's promise, Pitt didn't; Nebraska won 14-6. Rumor has it that Michelosen didn't speak to Beano for quite a while.

—When Beano was the ABC-TV flak and was stuck with other network suits in a massive traffic jam on the grounds of the U.S. Military Academy, he asked an M.P. directing traffic, "How'd you guys ever get us into Normandy?"

Beano grew up in Boston as the Boston Baked Bean, hence his nickname. When you say Beano, there is no need to mention his last name.

When his mother was asked why Beano never got married, she replied, "Who'd want to marry my son and spend her honeymoon at Pitt Stadium?"

Unforgettable Frank Howard

In the spring of 1978, I was one of the media "coaches" in Clemson's spring game. The honorary head coaches were Frank Howard (1940-69) and his predecessor, Jess Neely (1931-39). I still have the game program listing me as one of the assistant coaches—ahead of Danny Ford.

Frank Howard (Clemson University)

Clemson's quarterback that year was Steve Fuller. He was on our team, but Coach Charley Pell would only let him play one quarter for fear of injury.

With Fuller at the controls, we led 10-0. Without Fuller, we fell behind 17-10. But we got a nice drive going and had a first-and-goal at the 8-yard line with a couple of minutes left.

I was standing next to Coach Howard, who looked at me and drawled, "Ah believe ah'd just give the ball to the fullback a coupla times and kick a field goal."

I checked the scoreboard to make sure we were down by seven points, which we were. I didn't say anything.

A fourth-string quarterback named Mike Gasque lobbed the ball up for grabs in the end zone. Fortunately, it was caught by one of our players, All-American wideout Jerry Butler. Down 17-16, we sent fullback Marvin Sims up the middle for two points and won the game 18-17.

Coach Howard looked at me again and said, "Well, buddy, we came out all right, but ah believe ah'd have been a little more conservative—just give the ball to the fullback a coupla times and kick a field goal."

Now I had to say something.

"Coach, we were down by seven points. What the hell good would a field goal have done us?"

Howard looked at the scoreboard, then growled, "Goddammit, ah thought we wuz tied." A sheepish look came over his face, he elbowed me in the ribs and said, "You know, buddy, ah guess that's why ah ain't coaching no more."

Frank Howard was crude and coarse and crass and uncouth, etc., etc. He also was a Phi Beta Kappa in his undergraduate days at Alabama; if you lined up 100 people, Frank Howard, the Baron of Barlow Bend, Alabama, would have been the last one you guessed as a Phi Beta Kappa.

Frank Howard stories are legendary. When he was Clemson's athletic director, some students asked for money to form a crew. His reply turned out to be one of his most famous lines: "I ain't giving no money to no sport where you sit on your ass and go backwards."

Howard served as line coach under Jess Neely. When Neely went to Rice in 1940, the Clemson Athletic Council met to name a successor. A council member nominated Howard to be the new head coach. Howard, standing in the back of the room, said, "I second the nomination." He got the job.

The story goes that some members of the media visited Clemson and asked Howard if they could talk to a certain player.

"Jones," Howard hollered, "get your ass over here!"

When the writers questioned his choice of words, Howard allegedly replied:

"If this was Harvard, I'd say, 'Jones, please move your derriere over here as quickly as possible.' If this was Princeton, I'd say, 'Jones, kindly transport your posterior to this vicinity with all due haste.'

"But this ain't Harvard and this ain't Princeton, so I say, 'Jones, get your ass over here!'"

Howard was a few years ahead of Bear Bryant at Alabama. The two later became fast friends.

Once, as opposing coaches in an all-star game, they agreed that if either team was comfortably ahead, the losing coach would cross his arms as a signal to call off the dogs.

Bryant got the lead on Howard's team. Howard folded his arms. Bryant's team kept moving the ball. Howard moved down his sideline, emphatically folding his arms. Bryant ignored him.

Howard could take it no longer.

"Beah, Beah," he shouted. "You see me, you son of a bitch."

Bob Hope once performed in Clemson and stayed in the Holiday Inn on the banks of Lake Hartwell, at the time just about the tiny town's only motel.

The Clemson folk kept banging on his door, and finally Hope called Howard and said, "Frank, show me the town."

Howard picked him up and off they went. After driving through the town's only stoplight, Hope said, "Frank, I want you to show me the town."

"Bob," Howard said, "I'll be glad to back up and show it to you again."

Peahead Walker was the architect of one of the greatest recruiting coups in history.

In 1948, Wake Forest was recruiting a Pennsylvania lad named Bill George and he came down for a visit. Walker picked him up and gave him a tour of the campus—the Duke campus, which was much prettier than Wake's.

When George arrived in the fall for preseason practice, he surveyed his new surroundings and asked Walker, "Coach, where's that campus you showed me when I was here before."

"Oh," Walker lied, "that's the west campus. Freshmen have to live on the east campus."

Nevertheless, George hung around and became Wake Forest's first All-American.

On one occasion, Howard had Walker arrested prior to a game at Clemson. On Friday afternoon, as the Wake Forest team prepared to work out, Howard pointed at Walker and shouted, "There's the fugitive." A state policeman who was in on the gag handcuffed Walker to a telephone pole as Howard laughed his head off.

The next day, Walker didn't have his sideline pass and the guards wouldn't let him into the stadium. Walker yelled to his team captain, Pat Preston, to identify him.

"I've never seen him before in my life," said Preston, who was in on the prank. Walker finally got in, and Preston reportedly ran a record number of sprints when the team returned home.

Peterisms

Vince Gibson coached under Bill Peterson at Florida State. Consequently, he's full of Bill Peterson stories:

"One day in the summer . . . Peterson was always worried that you had to be at work at 8 o'clock in the summer and you had to work until 5. He'd gone on a fishing trip.

"So one day he called up ship to shore. He said, 'Ship to shore, ship to shore. Is Bob Harbison in?' 'Yeah, Coach, he's in; you want to talk to him?' 'No, I don't want to talk to him.' He said, 'Is Vince Gibson there?' 'Yeah, Vince is here; you want to talk to him?' 'No, I don't want to talk to him.' 'Is John Coatta there?' 'Yeah, Coach, he's here; you want to talk to John?' 'No, no.'

"'Is Don James there?' 'No, Coach, he's not here.' 'That's who I want to talk to.'

"He'd ask for somebody, if they weren't there, 'That's who I want to talk to.'"

"Coach Peterson, he hated the defense. He'd always make the offensive guys work until 1 or 2 in the morning. We had to be at work at 6 in the morning. [Don] James and I, we coached the defense, we'd sneak out about 10 at night and go home.

"One time we're in there at 6 o'clock in the morning, we're tired as all hell, and he comes in and gives us this defense, he could never get it all straight. He'd talk to Al Davis and he'd talk to Sid Gillman every day and he'd get something from them.

"But he didn't know much about defense; he'd get something down and he'd always screw it up. So he gave us this defense. We're playing Miami and we told him, 'We ain't gonna use that defense, Coach; it's no good. They use two tight ends, it's no good.'

"'Damn you, Gibson; damn you, James. If you don't stop 'em y'all are fired. Y'all are fired if you don't use my defense and you don't stop 'em, y'all are fired.'

"You had to argue and fight with him all the time. So he goes out and slams the door. Well, we go down there and we beat 'em 24-0. George Mira was the quarterback, we shut 'em out.

"After the game a bunch of sports writers came up to me and asked me, 'How did y'all do it? How did you shut 'em out?' "I said, 'Well, it's Coach Peterson's program, it's his discipline.' I was really braggin' on him. And he saw me talkin' to the sports writers, he came runnin' up there, 'Gibson, Gibson, you know how I feel about assistant coaches talkin' to sports writers.'

"Tom McEwen [of the *Tampa Tribune*] said, 'Pete, you dumb ass, here he is braggin' on you and buildin' you up and you come and make an ass out of yourself.'"

This is probably the most famous Peterson story:

"We were playing TCU and we got beat in a rain-storm and after the game he said, 'OK, I'll lead us in the Lord's Prayer. Get on your knees.' And he says, 'Now I lay me down to sleep . . .'

"All of a sudden he realized what he said and he said, 'Take it, Feely.' That was our little quarterback.

"We called those things 'Peterisms.'"

Some other "Peterisms":

—"The greatest thing just happened. I got indicted into the Florida Sports Hall of Fame."

—"You guys pair off in groups of threes, then line up in a circle."

—"Don't burn your bridges at both ends."

—To his players before a key game: "We can beat this team. All we have to do is capitalize on our mistakes."

—Excited and angered, making a point on his authority: "I'm the football coach around here — and don't you remember it!"

—Summing up a close game: "Whew! This was the cliff-dweller to end all cliff-dwellers."

—"He has a chronicle knee injury."

—At halftime: "Things are not going good out there and they've got our walls to the back. But we've got to keep our cools."

—While coaching the Houston Oilers, addressing his team on proper decorum when the national anthem is played: "I want you men standing on your helmets with the sidelines under your arms."

—Trying to pump up the Oilers: "I want you men thinking of one word, and one word only —Super Bowl."

Vince Gibson was on the Florida State staff the year the *Saturday Evening Post* ran a story that some flow, apparently due to crossed phone lines, allegedly overheard Bear Bryant and Georgia coach Wally Butts conspiring to fix a game.

"Butts called a lot of people," Gibson says, "which we found out later, and one of 'em was us at Florida State. We played Georgia. He called us and we were all in a big room, we didn't have offices, we were all in one big room with a bunch of desks around, all the assistant coaches.

"And he calls and Coach Pete [Bill Peterson] put him on the speakerphone and he was tellin' us, 'If I was playing Georgia, I'd watch for that Utah pass, that old shovel pass. If I was playing Georgia down on the goal line, I'd watch for 'em jumping that fullback up over the middle.'

"Then we found out he called about five or six teams. And we got investigated by the Senate, it was called the Kefauver Committee. And the coaches had to go down. Coach Pete was a nervous wreck. He thought all the phones were bugged. We had to talk in whispers.

"And nothing ever happened out of it, but it's just so ironic, we beat 'em 14-0 and they threw that shovel pass. It sounded like we were guilty as all get-out because we intercepted it. But what happened, they double-teamed the nose guard and he was flat on his back and the quarterback threw it behind the guy who was supposed to catch it and it landed right in our guy's stomach, and he was layin' on his back."

Bobby Bowden

This may come as a surprise, but Florida State wasn't always a great program.

In fact, before Bobby Bowden arrived in 1976, Florida State was right down there with the Kansas States, Northwesterns, Oregon States and other perennial doormats of that era.

There was nothing to indicate that little more than two decades later the Seminoles would have won two national championships and finished in the top four for

Bobby Bowden (Florida State University)

a record 13 consecutive seasons, each of which has produced 10 or more wins, another record.

For example:

—In the 46-29 Sugar Bowl win over Virginia Tech for the 1999 national championship, Florida State scored 28 points in the first half and 18 in the second half. In 1973, the last of Larry Jones' three seasons as head coach, the Seminoles never scored more than 17 points in a game —and they reached that figure only once. They scored 98 points for the entire season, barely twice what the current Seminoles scored against Virginia Tech.

—That 1973 season started a streak of 0-11, 1-10, 3-8 and 5-6 records, the middle two under Darrell Mudra, who coached from the press box, perhaps because he couldn't stand to be close to his players, and the last under a new kid on the block named Bowden, who had been run out of Morgantown, West Virginia.

—The leading scorer in 1973 and 1974 was placekicker Ahmet Askin with 20 and 26 points, respectively, FOR THE SEASON. Peter Warrick scored 18 points against Virginia Tech.

Before coming to Florida State, Bowden spent six seasons as head coach at West Virginia. Before that, he was head coach for four seasons at Samford University in Birmingham, Alabama, his hometown. Samford also was his alma mater, although it was known as Howard University way back then.

Few people know this, but Bowden also was a head coach before Samford. He coached at South Georgia Junior College in Douglas as part of a two-man staff. The party of the second part, the defensive coordinator, was Vince Gibson, later head coach at Louisville and Kansas State.

"I had graduated from Florida State and I took a job in St. Augustine, Florida, right on the beach," Gibson recalls. "I was making $4,500 a year. He drives down, has dinner with me, all of us went to high school together—my first wife, me, Ann (Mrs. Bowden) and Bobby."

"Bobby offered me a job at $3,600 a year and I had to teach the girls' phys. ed. because Ann wouldn't let him teach the girls. He talked me into going up there. There was a 50-cent toll bridge to get back home and he had to drive over a hundred miles out of the way 'cause he didn't have 50 cents and he had too much pride to borrow the 50 cents from me.

"We had more fun. That was the best three years I ever spent in coaching. Just he and I were the coaches. He was the head football coach. I coached basketball, girls' basketball and track, he coached baseball."

"One year we gave too many scholarships. He was worried to death about what he was gonna do. The first game we got upset, got beat, so he called them all in there. Six of the seven linemen I was coaching were older'n me;

they'd all just come back from the Korean War. He says, 'OK, how many guys broke training this week?'

"About 15 hands stuck up. He said, 'OK, you guys are all off scholarship at the end of the semester.' We couldn't get a guy to volunteer for anything after that. It all worked out, we didn't have to cut nobody.

"And today, every other year, Bobby goes back to South Georgia. They have a reunion of all the South Georgia kids from 1958, the last year we were there.

"He made $4,500, I made $3,600; this is a year now, not a month. We both lived in a deserted barracks, it was a deserted Air Force field. I paid $15 a month and he paid $25 'cause he had a double. The first time my mama saw where I lived, she cried. I had six johns in my bathroom. It was an old barracks, you know.

Futility U.

That's how *Sports Illustrated* described Kansas State before Bill Snyder became head coach in 1989.

Other than the fact that they hadn't won a game in two seasons, how bad were the Wildcats before Snyder arrived? So bad that the school's first mascot, a wildcat named Touchdown I, lost a battle with a porcupine.

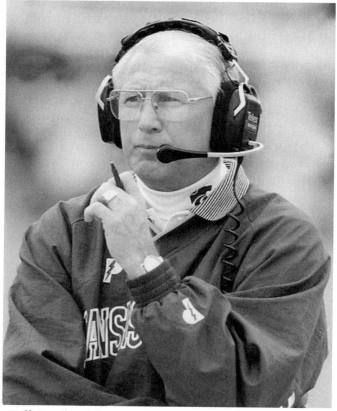

Bill Snyder (Associated Press)

In 1922, Coach Charley Bachman asked alumni to consider donating an actual wildcat to serve as a mascot. Herbert R. Groome and John E. McCoy, veterinarians in Twin Falls, Idaho, donated Touchdown I shortly after the animal was nursed back to health under their care.

Seems Touchdown I had an encounter with a porcupine, and its face and throat were punctured by numerous quills. Touchdown I never fully recovered and died of pneumonia shortly after arriving on campus.

The mascots no longer attend K-State games. Touchdown XI, the current mascot, resides at Manhattan's Sunset Zoo.

Before starting a long winning streak in 1990, Kansas State's homecoming record was 5-34-2. That's unthinkable. On homecoming, you schedule Topeka Junior High, someone like that.

Quick Quiz: Bill Snyder's record in his first 11 years at Kansas State was well over .650, but he didn't surpass the .500 mark until the final game of his fifth season (27-26-1). Who was the last Kansas State coach to leave with an overall winning record?

Answer: Hall of Famer Lynn "Pappy" Waldorf, who led the Wildcats to a 7-2-1 mark in 1934, his only season as head coach, and then left for greener pastures. Between Waldorf and Snyder, K-State went through Wes Fry, Hobbs Adams, Ward Haylett, Lud Fiser, Sam Francis, Ralph Graham, Bill Meek, Bus Mertes, Doug Weaver, Vince Gibson, Ellis Rainsberger, Jim Dickey and Stan Parrish. Fry, Adams, Haylett, Weaver, Gibson and Parrish all won their first games before the roof fell in. Parrish was 2-4 at one point in his first season and then went 0-26-1.

"When I took the job, they hadn't won a game in two-and-a-half years," says Gibson. "When I first came there, freshmen weren't eligible. Only reason I took the job, I really didn't want the job, but I told 'em all the things they needed to do to win, I was 32 years old and I wanted a head job.

"I said you got to build a stadium. In the South we all had athletic dorms. You got to build an athletic dorm, and you got to have a swimming pool with it. I said you got to have a built-in steam bath. I came back and they offered me the job. I said, you remember all those things I told you? They said you can have all those things.

"I found out they were trying to kick 'em out of the Big Eight 'cause they had this old stadium, they averaged less than 10,000 a game.

"We won the first game after they'd lost 23 straight, beat Colorado State. We came home after the game and, boy, they had signs, they thought I was the greatest coach in the country. They had 'Vince walks on water' signs, the governor was there, everybody was all excited. We lost nine in a row after that.

After one game there was a sign, "Can Vince swim?"

"A story I've never told," Gibson says.

"I got a call from a guy one time in Vegas and this guy told me that . . . we were playing Nebraska for the Big Eight championship in 1970, we were 5-1, they were 5-0, they had Oklahoma left to play. If we'd have beaten them, we'd at least tied for it.

"We'd played 'em three straight times. They'd beaten us 16-14, we'd beaten them 12-0, they'd beaten us 10-7.

"This guy calls me up, a guy that I knew, a friend of a friend of Don James when he went to school at Miami. He'd moved to Vegas and he called me and he said, 'You know, the line's come out and y'all are 17-point underdogs. Seventeen-point underdogs? How can that be? We'd won four or five straight ball games. And he said, 'They bought the back judge.'

"I said, 'You're kidding, they don't buy the back judge, those things don't happen.' So I called the Big Eight office. A guy named John Waldorf was the head of officials, and he said, 'Aw, that ain't happening, that ain't happening.' I said, 'I'm just telling you what happened.'

"Score's 14-7, about two minutes to go in the half. We fake a field goal and got a guy wide open in the end zone. Their guy just dives over the top of him, the ball hits him in the back, it's definitely pass interference, they don't call nothing. My guy jumps up and hollers at the official, 'What do you mean?' Throws him out of the game. My best player, Mike Montgomery.

"The score is 17-7 in the second half and we're driving down again. We throw a slant-in pass, they clothesline the receiver, break his nose, the ball bounces on the ground, they caught it on the first bounce, run it down to our 5-yard line, they call it an interception. They go in and score. They end up beating us 47-13.

"After the game . . . it was so obvious you couldn't ignore it. So they questioned the official, he was a junior high principal from Des Moines, Iowa, and he admitted that he took $10,000. They called me and said don't ever say anything about this, what good would it do? It'd just hurt football. I never said a word about that. They kicked him out of officiating.

"That taught me a lesson. During all the years, there's more games won and lost because of officiating than anything."

The Coach, Lee Corso

One of my favorite people—and closest friends—is Lee Corso, who coached at Louisville (1969-72), Indiana (1973-82) and Northern Illinois (most of 1984, before he grew tired of DeKalb, Illinois, the barbed-wire capital of the world).

Lee Corso (Indiana University)

Corso's antics when he coached at Louisville have been well documented—the turkey mascot, riding an elephant in a parade, waving a white towel of surrender at Memphis State coach Billy "Spook" Murphy during a 69-19 shellacking in his first year at Louisville (1969). He never lost to Memphis State again.

Corso also used to drive several miles out of his way en route to work to remind himself there were people worse off than he was.

One of Corso's favorite players was Francis Ayandele. Even super trivia buffs probably never heard of him. Neither had Corso, until . . .

"One day I was sitting in the office at the University of Louisville in 1969. I heard a knock on the door and there's a guy 6-8, about 120 pounds, standing there.

"He says, 'Coach?' I said, 'Yeah.' He said, 'My name's Francis Ayandele.' I said, 'Yeah, Francis, what do you do?' He said, 'I'm a soccer player, but I want to keek football.' I said, 'C'mon, Francis, you gotta be kidding me.' He said, 'No, I show you.'

"I said, 'Okay, just come back tomorrow at noon. I don't want anybody to see you. You come at noon, everybody'll be at lunch and you can kick for me.'

"He came back the next day. I put the ball down, he went— Boom!—he kicked the thing over everything. It went outta sight. I said, 'Whoa, this kid's my kicker.'

"This was Thursday. I said, 'Come back on Saturday, the game's on Saturday.' He had never seen a game. So I helped him get dressed, took him out there, everything worked out fine and we were gonna kick off.

"So he lines up to kick off. The other team [Drake] gets in a huddle, my team gets in a huddle. He's lookin' at me and he waves at me and I wave at him and all of a sudden he starts running. Da-dee, da-dee, da-dee. Boom! He kicked the ball off before the game started.

"He kicked it out of the end zone. Francis is running down the field and everybody's running onto the field. There's a fight; it was the damnedest fight you've ever seen, blood all over the place, 'cause they're still in the huddle and our guys are beating them down there.

"The referee says to me, 'What's going on?' I said, 'He's a new guy, I'll talk to him.'

"I said, 'Francis, don't kick it till you see me go, thweet—then you go.' He said, 'Okay.' So we line up again and Francis is watching. They're in a huddle, all their heads are looking back at Francis, they think he's gonna kick it off too soon again. So finally he starts going and—Boom!—he kicks it off and he's running down the field looking at me—6-8, 120 pounds and he's waving at me. I said, 'Oh, no.'

"This big guy had a big bead on him and he [Francis] is looking at me, waving, and all of sudden—Pow!—the guy hits him right in the mouth, knocks his helmet off, he's knocked out.

"I ran out on the field. I said, 'Francis?' He said, 'Coach, you don't tell me they can hit me.' I said, 'Hey, Francis, I forgot to tell you that.'

"In about the third or fourth quarter, it was a real close game [24-24 final], and he taps me on the shoulder. It's fourth-and-one. I said, 'What's going on?' He had a little camera around his neck, he was taking pictures of me. I said, 'What the hell are you doing?' He said, 'I want a picture of you, Coach. Nobody remember me in this game. I want to make sure my friends know I play the game.'

"So he's on the sideline posing with me in the fourth quarter of a close game, taking pictures. Francis was a real good guy."

Corso not only was something of a character himself, but seemed to attract them like flies to honey. Like Scott Marcus, Louisville's punter from 1970 to 1972.

"I made a speech at the freshman orientation," Corso remembers, "and I walked out of the Student Union and there was a telephone booth and there was a guy looked like he was living in this telephone booth. Long hair, hippie guy, and he had flowers in his ears and no shoes on.

"And he said, 'Coach.' I looked at him. He said, 'Come over here.' I said, 'No way.' He said, 'Come over here.' I went over there and I said, 'What's your name?' He said, 'Scott Marcus. I want to help the team.' I said, 'I bet you do.' And he said, 'I'm a punter.' I said, 'Come on, come on, you can't punt.' He said, 'I punt barefooted.' I said, 'You're crazy.'

"I took him on the field and he kicked the ball like crazy. I said, 'You're now my punter.' Against Marshall, it's fourth-and-about-15 and we're in punt formation on our own 20-yard line.

The guy snaps to Scott, Marcus gets the ball, runs over and throws it to me. I catch it and everybody's going crazy, we faked a punt. I says, 'What the hell are you doing? Why'd you throw the ball to me?' He said, 'I looked around and you were the only guy open.'

"But he was a hell of a punter. His dad owned a shoe company somewhere on Long Island, but he never wore shoes. Scott Marcus, great kid."

Herschel Nissenson (left), Lee Corso (right) and golf partners. (Photo courtesy of Herschel Nissenson).

The American Football Coaches Association no longer holds a golf tournament. It began in Arkansas in the 1960s and moved from Cherokee Village to Bella Vista to Hot Springs Village, then to Shreveport, Louisiana, for a year and to Irving, Texas, for more than a decade.

I was first invited in 1973 to Hot Springs Village, a luxurious retirement community. Denne Freeman, the AP's Southwest sports editor based in Dallas, had gone a few times and, knowing my love for country music, had told me that one of the annual highlights was a country singer Darrell Royal brought every year. A different one each year.

We gathered in Darrell's town house (Two couples shared each town house). Darrell introduced a fellow whom he described as a top songwriter who was just starting to make it as a recording artist.

"Please welcome Willie Nelson," he said.

Willie came out in his cutoff jeans and tank top playing the same guitar he still plays, the famous one with a hole in the body. He serenaded us all night long—and I mean ALL night long. A concert like that today would cost a million dollars or more.

As luck would have it, my wife and I shared a town house with Lee and Betsy Corso. I had met Lee earlier when he spoke at the AFCA's annual convention in Hollywood, California, and made some remarks that rocked the old-fogey coaching establishment.

One night, sitting in the town house, Lee, who was about to begin his first season at Indiana, told me, "I'm gonna hire a woman coach."

"Yeah, right," I said.

"No, I mean it," Lee said. "I don't mean someone to coach on the field, but someone to act as a liaison with the parents."

I wrote the story and it got more attention than anything Corso ever did. A year or so later I was in Bloomington, Indiana, and Lee showed me some of the "fan mail" he had received. "You male chauvinist pig" was among the kindest ones.

Corso hired Elizabeth "Buzz" Kurpius, and she directed the athletic department's academic affairs for a quarter of a century before retiring as an associate athletic director.

In 1999, Iowa held a roast for Hayden Fry, who retired after two decades as the Hawkeyes' head coach. The festivities were emceed by ESPN's Lee Corso, who was the opponent in Fry's first game at Iowa (Indiana at home on September 8, 1979).

The Hawkeyes built a 26-3 halftime lead and were 30 minutes from giving Fry a game to remember; instead, it turned into a nightmare to forget.

Corso, whose coaching antics were somewhat off-the-wall, to say the least, told his players at halftime that they could rally for the biggest comeback in Indiana history or get dressed, go home and forfeit the game.

Corso came out of the locker room and told the officials, "Get ready to notify the Big Ten office. We might forfeit."

"You can't forfeit," he was told.

"Why not?" Corso said. "We're gonna get beat anyway."

They didn't. The Hoosiers rallied to win 30-26 on a 66-yard pass from Tim Clifford to Lonnie Johnson with 58 seconds remaining, still the biggest comeback in Indiana history.

Afterward, Corso told Fry, "Coach, you have a five-year contract. I needed this game more than you did."

Footnote: Corso's son, Steve, an Indiana wideout, went deep down the sideline, and the Iowa safety bit, leaving Johnson wide open for the winning touchdown. The safety's name? Bob Stoops, now Oklahoma's head coach.

A few years ago, I ran into Bob Chmiel, a Notre Dame assistant coach who was on Corso's staff at Northern Illinois in 1984.

"Have you ever seen Corso's organizational book?" Chmiel said. I said I hadn't.

Chmiel said Corso was so organized, he had a coach assigned to supply candles in the event of a power failure and another coach responsible for the matches.

I asked Corso if those things were true.

"Yeah," he said. "I also had a coach assigned to make sure there was toilet paper in the coaches' john."

When Lee Corso coached at Indiana and it came time to order office furniture, he always made sure his desk was a foot longer than Bobby Knight's.

Corso called me one weekend after his team had been beaten by Ohio State.

"Guess what," he chortled, "I made Woody (Hayes) throw the ball to beat me."

The Heisman—Trophy and Tragedy

The late Les Horvath, Ohio State's 1944 Heisman Trophy winner, used to joke about his early days as a dentist in Los Angeles after a three-year stint in professional football.

Seems Horvath's wife couldn't understand why he was so addicted to a bronze sculpture depicting a running back with a football tucked under his left arm and straight-arming a would-be tackler with his right. She

The Heisman Trophy (Downtown Athletic Club)

wanted to (a) throw it out, or (b) use it as a doorstop. Horvath explained that it was a unique trophy and had been awarded barely a dozen times.

Shortly thereafter, the Horvaths visited the Glenn Davises, and there on the mantel was Davis' 1946 Heisman Trophy. The following night they were guests of the Tom Harmons and, sure enough, there on the mantel was Harmon's 1940 Heisman.

When they got home, Mrs. Horvath looked at her husband and snorted, "What do you mean 'unique'; all our friends have one."

Jay Berwanger, the first Heisman winner when he played for the University of Chicago in 1935, didn't use the 25-pound trophy as a doorstop.

"I could not find a suitable place, a proper place, for it at my fraternity house," he recalled, "so I asked my aunt to look after it until I could. She used it for a doorstop."

If you want to nitpick, Berwanger didn't win the Heisman. He won what was then called the Downtown Athletic Club Trophy. John Heisman was director of athletics at the DAC, and upon his death early in 1936, the trophy was renamed in his honor.

And it's ironic that the first recipient was from the Windy City because there are few places on earth windier than the strip between the front door of the DAC and Hudson River across the street—roughly the length of a football field away—in lower Manhattan.

The Heisman Trophy is still unique. Ohio State tailback Archie Griffin, the only two-time winner (1974-75), kept one of his Heismans on his TV set, explaining

John Heisman (SPI Archives)

that if you wanted to watch television, you had to look at his trophy.

"It is class," 1984 winner Doug Flutie said of the Heisman. "It opens doors for you for the rest of your life."

When Harmon received the 1940 Heisman, he called his mother to the dais and handed her the trophy, forgetting how much it weighed. Mrs. Harmon almost fell down trying to hold it.

Johnny Lattner, Notre Dame's 1953 winner, had his trophy on display for a time at a Chicago restaurant. Angelo Bertelli, another Notre Damer and the 1943 winner, would lend his trophy to a friend who operated a clothing store to help promote the new fall lines.

Bertelli and the 1942 winner, Georgia's Frankie Sinkwich, didn't receive their trophies right away. The war was on and there was a shortage of

Doug Flutie (Boston College)

metal. At one point, the Heisman Committee asked DAC members to bring in contributions for 25 pounds of scrap metal so a trade could be made with authorities for a trophy. But any metal was hard to come by, so Sinkwich and Bertelli were given certificates and received their trophies later.

Clint Frank of Yale, the 1938 winner, was away on vacation one year when his home caught fire. The first thing the firemen rescued was his Heisman Trophy.

"Smart men," Frank said. "I sent them a case of scotch."

Not many Heisman winners have had all-pro careers, but the Heisman is awarded for accomplishments in college and isn't based on pro potential. Too many members of the media seem ready to knock a Heisman winner when he doesn't become an all-pro.

The 1997 Heisman went to a primarily defensive player for the first time, cornerback Charles Woodson of Michigan. Having been fairly close to the Heisman for the better part of three decades, I kept getting the impression the voters were looking someday to honor a defensive player. However, Woodson was aided by three things—(1) he also played some on offense, (2) *Sports Illustrated* ran an article shamelessly promoting him just as the Heisman ballots went out, and (3) he had a great game against Ohio State on national television, including a 37-yard reception that set up Michigan's first touchdown, a 78-yard punt return for another TD, a key pass breakup late in the game and an interception. Before that game, Woodson trailed Tennessee quarterback Peyton Manning by about nine percentage points; after the game, he jumped to a lead of about 7 1/2 points, and disappointed Tennesseans burned up the phone lines to New York.

Pittsburgh defensive end Hugh Green was runner-up to South Carolina's George Rogers in 1980 after the school conducted a strong campaign, sending out posters with a picture of the Jolly Green Giant (remember him?) superimposed on Green's face. Yale's Larry Kelley (1936) and Notre Dame's Leon Hart (1949) were two-way ends. Other defenders need not apply.

I wasn't surprised when George Rogers, then with the New Orleans Saints, said his goal for an upcoming season was "to gain 1,500 or 2,000 yards, whichever comes first."

When Rogers won the 1980 Heisman, much of his thunder was being usurped by a Georgia freshman named Herschel Walker.

I covered the South Carolina-Georgia game in Athens, but went through Columbia, South Carolina, to do a story on Rogers.

Herschel Walker (University of Georgia)

139

I had met Rogers twice previously. The first time was the previous December, when South Carolina played Missouri in the Hall of Fame Bowl in Birmingham; the second time was eight months later, when he was part of a cross-country tour sponsored by the NCAA and ABC-TV. Both times he was introduced to me, told who I was and what I did and we talked for an hour or so.

Now it was October 1980, and on the practice field in Columbia George Rogers was introduced to me for the third time in 10 months. Coach Jim Carlen excused Rogers from the last few minutes of practice so I could talk to him.

As we walked off the field, just to make small talk, I said to Rogers, "George, I guess my name doesn't sit too well with you these days since I have the same name as that running back at Georgia."

And George Rogers, who had just been introduced to me for the third time in less than a year, looked at me and said, "Your name Walker?"

The televised Heisman announcement and the annual banquet a few days later are festive occasions. But Heisman history also is filled with tragedy.

Nile Kinnick of Iowa, for whom that university's football stadium is named, won the Heisman in 1939 as war clouds were gathering over much of the world. In his Heisman acceptance speech, Kinnick thanked God that he had been born in America, "where they have football fields, instead of Europe, where they have battlefields."

Kinnick became a pilot attached to an aircraft carrier in the Caribbean. In June 1943, he crash-landed his fighter plane in the sea and was never found.

Minnesota's Bruce Smith, the 1941 winner, died only 26 years later after a long illness. Ernie Davis of Syracuse (1961) was struck down by leukemia shortly after signing an $80,000 contract with the Cleveland Browns. He died in 1963 without ever playing a professional game.

Georgia Tech has never had a Heisman winner, although John Heisman coached there. But Georgia Tech can claim as much Heisman misery as any school. Four times a Tech player has finished among the top five in the Heisman balloting. Two of them died tragically and much too soon — Clint Castleberry, third in 1942 as a freshman (The only other freshman to finish that high was Georgia's Herschel Walker in 1980), and Eddie Prokop, fifth in

Clint Castleberry (Georgia Tech)

1943. Ironically, they were teammates in 1942. Billy Lothridge, runner-up to Roger Staubach in 1963, died of a heart attack in 1996 at the age of 54. All-American quarterback Joe Hamilton, the 1999 runner-up, wasn't drafted until the seventh and last round.

I knew of Eddie Prokop because he played with the New York Yankees in the old All-American Football Conference. I had never heard of Clint Castleberry until I read a story in the Georgia Tech media guide a few years ago.

A single-wing tailback, Clint Castleberry didn't start his first college game in 1942 as Georgia Tech beat Auburn 15-0. Yet, Notre Dame scout Wayne Millner told Coach Frank Leahy that "the most dangerous runner in America" would invade South Bend the following weekend.

"A crazed jackrabbit" was the way one writer described him. Another noted that "Tech's Old Guard . . . hailed the freshman Castleberry as the fanciest runner to hit the Flats since they have forgotten when."

A straight-A student at Atlanta's Boys High, Castleberry never played in a losing football game in three varsity seasons there. Navy and Notre Dame considered recruiting him, but backed off after learning he was only 5-9 and 155 pounds. Both schools would regret their decision.

Castleberry wavered between Georgia and Georgia Tech, choosing the latter school because he was in love with a local girl.

The legendary Bobby Dodd, an assistant coach at Tech under Bill Alexander in 1942, always maintained that Castleberry would "have probably been an All-American for three years and been the greatest back in Georgia Tech history . . . he was a great football player. He might have been the best of them all, had he lived. But what is more important is this: He was a great boy—gentle and brave, manly, yet sweet."

"Ty Cobb, Jeb Stuart, Clint Castleberry—only heroes I ever had," former Tech player and coach Pepper Rodgers once said.

The legend of Clint Castleberry began in high school when he played against Central High of Charlotte, North Carolina, led by Charlie "Choo Choo" Justice, and scored the first five times he touched the ball. In his senior year, despite playing less than half of each game, he averaged 171 yards a game rushing and scored 102 points.

Because of the war, the Southeastern Conference (Tech was a member then) ruled freshmen eligible to play in 1942. One week after beginning his career against Auburn, Castleberry, who played both ways, recovered a fumble at the Notre Dame 27 and then threw an eight-yard pass for Tech's first touchdown. In the fourth quarter, a Castleberry punt return set up the winning touchdown as Georgia Tech won for the first time ever in South Bend.

Three weeks later, Castleberry intercepted a pass against Navy and returned it 95 yards for a touchdown as Tech won 21-0. He even ran out the clock with a 51-yard run.

Georgia, with Frank Sinkwich, who won the 1942 Heisman, and Charlie Trippi, was ranked No. 1, and Tech was climbing, defeating Duke, Kentucky, Alabama and

Florida en route to a 9-0 record and a No. 2 national ranking. But one game before their meeting, Georgia was upset by Auburn, and Castleberry suffered a knee injury against Florida.

Castleberry reinjured his knee in a 34-0 loss to Georgia and played sparingly in a 14-7 Cotton Bowl loss to Texas. Six weeks later, he enlisted in the Army Air Corps.

On November 7, 1944, Franklin Delano Roosevelt was overwhelmingly elected to an unprecedented fourth term in the White House. A few hours before the polls opened, two "Marauder" bombers took off from Roberts Field in Nigeria, continuing their ferrying run up the West African coast toward Dakar, Senegal. The co-pilot of one was Lt. Clinton Dillard Castleberry Jr. of Atlanta, Georgia. The bombers were never heard from again.

American planes, aided by the Royal Navy and Royal Air Force, searched for six days. The War Department gave up hope on November 23, changing Castleberry's status from "missing" to "killed," though the only evidence was some unidentified wreckage spotted on the ocean by an RAF plane.

Meanwhile, Eddie Prokop came to Georgia Tech by way of Cleveland, Ohio, and the Baylor School in Chattanooga, Tennessee. It was said that he made an impact on Atlanta like no Ohioan since Gen. William Tecumseh Sherman.

In 1943, with Castleberry gone off to war, Prokop was Tech's star, a big, fast triple-threat back. He led the Yellow Jackets past LSU and Steve Van Buren 42-0. He completed 11 straight passes in a 33-0 rout of Tulane.

On January 1, 1944, Prokop engineered a late 79-yard drive as Tech rallied from an 18-7 deficit to beat Tulsa 20-18 in the Sugar Bowl. Prokop's 199 rushing yards remained a Sugar Bowl record until broken by Pitt's Tony Dorsett in 1977.

Prokop gave up his senior year to enter the navy, later playing pro ball. On Memorial Day 1955, he died of a brain hemorrhage after complaining of severe headaches. He was 33 years old.

Bowling For Dollars

If you think 23 bowls, the 1999 number, is too many, how about a moment of silence for the dear departed.

The NCAA lists 27 contests that are no longer with us as "former major bowl games." Alphabetically, they were the Alamo Bowl in San Antonio (not to be confused with the current Alamo Bowl in San Antonio), the All American Bowl in Birmingham, the Aviation Bowl in Dayton, the Bacardi Bowl in Havana, the Bluebonnet Bowl in Houston, the Bluegrass Bowl in Louisville, the California Bowl in Fresno, the Camellia Bowl in Lafayette,

Orange Bowl program

Louisiana, the Cherry Bowl in Pontiac, Michigan, the Delta Bowl in Memphis, the Dixie Bowl in Birmingham, the Dixie Classic in Dallas, the Fort Worth Classic.

Also, the Freedom Bowl in Anaheim, California, the Garden State Bowl in East Rutherford, New Jersey, the Gotham Bowl in New York City, the Great Lakes Bowl in Cleveland, the Harbor Bowl in San Diego, the Los Angeles Christmas Festival, the Mercy Bowl in Los Angeles, the Oil Bowl in Houston, the Pasadena Bowl (where else?), the Presidential Cup in College Park, Maryland, the Raisin Bowl in Fresno, the Salad Bowl in Phoenix, the San Diego East-West Christmas Classic and the Shrine Bowl in Little Rock.

The Bluebonnet had the longest run—29 years; 11 others were one-time affairs. Of those, the strangest surely was the Bacardi Bowl, also referred to as the Rhumba Bowl, on January 1, 1937, between Alabama Polytechnic Institute and Villanova University.

Alabama Poly has gone on to bigger and better things, but is still located in the sleepy little Southern village of Auburn.

There weren't many bowl games back then, although Alabama Poly was one year away from an Orange Bowl date. These days, the Loveliest Village of the Plains boasts Tommy Tuberville; then, the head man was Jack Meagher, known around Lee County as the Saviour of the South.

Meagher inherited a 5-5 team and promptly went 2-8 in 1934. In 1935, however, he turned it around to 8-2, and in 1936 the Tigers were 7-2-2, with six shutouts. In November of that year, Cuban president Miguel Gomez, trying to do something about his administration's poor public image, was talked into hosting a weeklong sports festival as a goodwill gesture. The Columbia University basketball team had agreed to play a Cuban team, and Olympic track star Jesse Owens agreed to race a horse in a 100-yard dash, but the highlight of the festival was to be a football game between two American college teams.

Overtures were made to Alabama, which wasn't interested. It was suggested to the festival's organizers that there was another team in the state a couple of hours from Tuscaloosa (Even in those days Auburn played second fiddle). But who would Auburn play? Since Cuba was a country of many Catholics, Villanova was invited.

Over the years, teams have had well-documented problems with bowl games. For instance, Nebraska refused to take off from Lincoln in 1962 until the Gotham Bowl deposited its guarantee in a bank. But the problem that faced Auburn and Villanova was unique—the Cuban government was overthrown in a bloodless coup, and Gomez was replaced by a former army corporal named Fulgencio Batista (Fidel Castro was only nine years old). His aides convinced Batista to go ahead with the festival.

Elmer Salter, who served as Auburn's unofficial sports publicist, went to Havana to advance the game and found a nation in turmoil and tension. Once, at the home of a local sports writer, Salter was greeted by a man with a shotgun.

Shortly before the Auburn team was scheduled to depart for Havana, Meagher called Salter and said the university hadn't received its guarantee, estimated at anywhere from $7,500 to $10,000. The Cubans quickly handed over a check, although it was learned later that a check had indeed been sent from New York to Opelika, Alabama, but was never received because the school banked in Auburn, the next town over.

With the money in hand, the Auburn team took a train from Opelika to Tampa, then boarded the S.S. *Cuba* and sailed to Key West and then on to Havana. Some players spent a lot of time at the ship's rail, and not just to admire the water.

When the game finally kicked off in a baseball stadium under a blazing sun before a reported crowd of less than 9,000 (The NCAA generously lists it as 12,000), Auburn took a 7-0 lead in the first quarter on a 40-yard run by Billy Hitchcock, who later became a major league baseball player and manager. The Tigers held on, using several quick kicks to get out of dangerous field position.

In the waning moments, however, Auburn tried it one time too often. Villanova blocked it, recovered in the end zone and the game ended 7-7. It was the beginning of an Auburn-Villanova series which ran the next six years, but it was both the beginning and end of the Bacardi Bowl, the only true bowl game ever played on foreign soil.

You've heard of fifth-year seniors, and even an occasional sixth-year senior, but have you ever heard of anyone who played in five bowl games? Real bowl games, not all-star contests like the Senior Bowl or Hula Bowl.

The answer is former Iowa quarterback Chuck Long, who was inducted into the College Football Hall of Fame in 1999 and left the Iowa staff after the 1999 season to become quarterbacks coach at Oklahoma.

When Long was an Iowa freshman in 1981, the Big Ten had a new rule that you couldn't redshirt freshmen. However, Big Ten coaches made sure freshmen got some snaps before being redshirted as sophomores.

"That was their plan for me," Long says. "I didn't take many snaps as a freshman. I only played in one quarter of one ball game, and then we went to the Rose Bowl and I took the last two snaps of the game. We were getting beat pretty soundly (Washington 28-0), so Hayden [Coach Fry] threw me in and said, 'Hey, why don't you get on national TV and get a little playing time.'

"The next year, the Big Ten thought that was a silly rule, so they threw it out. A handful of us in the Big Ten got cheated out of a year because we got very limited playing time [as freshmen].

"Unfortunately for Hayden's plan, I ended up starting my sophomore year. As a sophomore, we went to the Peach Bowl; as a junior, we went to the Gator Bowl; as a senior, we went to the Freedom Bowl. Those were my four years right there.

"Iowa, along with the rest of the Big Ten, petitioned the NCAA and said, 'Hey, there's a handful of players in this league that got cheated because of that rule.' The NCAA came back and said okay, if you want an extra year you can have an extra year. So I was a senior twice at Iowa and we went to the Rose Bowl the next year.

"I took a snap in five bowl games; it'll never happen again."

Games of the Century

I don't know how many Games of the Century there were in the 20th century, but I saw three of them.

I expect there will be some in the 21st century, but they'll have to go some to rival my three.

I was lucky. The first national game I ever covered remains the best—Nebraska at Oklahoma, Thanksgiving Day 1971.

No. 1 Nebraska (10-0) beat No. 2 Oklahoma (9-0) 35-31. That was the order in which they finished, too, with No. 3 Colorado giving the Big Eight an unprecedented and unequaled 1-2-3 sweep of the polls. The lead changed hands four times, and it was one of those closer-than-the-score-would-indicate games.

At the time, though, it was only the Game of the Decade. It has since become my personal Game of the Century because almost every other such billing has fallen short, although two others came close. Nebraska had won the 1970 national championship and would repeat in 1971. This wasn't one of those Tom Osborne-Barry Switzer duels. It was Nebraska's Bob Devaney against Oklahoma's Chuck Fairbanks, although Osborne and Switzer were on the respective staffs.

How big was it? Devaney, covering all bases, had his players' food flown in from Lincoln to Norman.

Nebraska was led by quarterback Jerry Tagge, bruising tailback Jeff Kinney and a will-o'-the-wisp wingback/kick returner named Johnny Rodgers, who would go on to win the 1972 Heisman Trophy. Rodgers scored the game's first touchdown on a 72-yard punt return; Kinney

Devaney carried after Orange Bowl
(University of Nebraska)

rushed for 174 yards and scored Nebraska's other four
TDs, including the game-winner with less than two minutes left and his jersey in tatters to cap a 74-yard, 12-play
drive. Oklahoma also scored four touchdowns, but added
only a field goal while Nebraska had Rodgers' glittering
punt return. The game was so well played that there was
only one penalty.

Oklahoma was in its second season of the wishbone
offense with Jack Mildren, later the lieutenant governor,
running the show and halfback Greg Pruitt running here,
there and everywhere. The Cornhuskers tried to neutral-
ize Pruitt and, to compensate, moved safety Bill Kosch
to cornerback and played him man-on-man against wide
receiver Jon Harrison, an assignment he wasn't used to.
Devaney acknowledged that that was a mistake; Mildren
threw two touchdown passes to Harrison.

In the *Omaha World-Herald*, Wally Provost's game story began: "In what surely must stand as one of the most stirring dramas in the 102 years of college football . . ."

Despite all the offensive pyrotechnics, it was Nebraska's defense that made the Cornhuskers one of the best teams ever—and Oklahoma wasn't far behind. Nebraska tackle Larry Jacobson won the Outland Trophy —and he was only the Huskers' third-best defensive lineman. Nose guard Rich Glover won the Outland and Lombardi in 1972, and end Willie Harper went on to NFL stardom. The 'Huskers were so good that Monte Johnson, a backup tackle, never started, but was a regular on the Oakland Raiders' 1977 Super Bowl champs. And against the nation's best defense, Oklahoma wishboned its way to 467 yards. It wasn't enough.

Before Nebraska-Oklahoma, there had been classics like Texas-Arkansas, 1969 (the Big Shootout), Notre Dame-Michigan State, 1966 (the Game of the Year), Notre Dame-Army, 1946 (an earlier Game of the Century), Michigan-Minnesota, 1940 (the Battle of the Giants), TCU-SMU, 1935 (the Aerial Circus). Ho-hum!

Since that memorable day in 1971, there have been other games that aspired to be Games of the Century. There was Nebraska-Miami in the 1983 Orange Bowl, Miami-Florida State in 1987 and again in 1992, Miami-Notre Dame in 1988, Miami-Penn State in the 1986 Fiesta Bowl, Penn State-Alabama in the Sugar Bowl, a few more Nebraska-Oklahoma gems and a number of Bo-Woody Michigan-Ohio State Paleozoic-type Neanderthals.

But for me, there are two other games that stand above the rest. One was the day after Thanksgiving 1984. Miami, the 1983 national champion, and quarterback Bernie Kosar vs. Boston College and quarterback Doug Flutie in the Orange Bowl. With 28 seconds left, Melvin Bratton scored his fourth touchdown for a 45-41 Miami lead.

Safe? You should live so long. Flutie, who completed 34 of 46 passes for 472 yards and three touchdowns (Kosar

Doug Flutie (Boston College)

was 25 of 38 for 447 yards and two TDs), saved the best for last. On the final play, after scrambling for what seemed an eternity, he hurled his famous 48-yard "Hail Mary" from his own 36-yard line to a leaping Gerard Phelan in the end zone for a 47-45 B.C. win.

Almost as exciting as Flutie's pass was the sight of Cotton Bowl head Jim Brock and his disappearing cigar. Brock and B.C. athletic director Bill Flynn—a former president of the NCAA, no less—had conspired, well in advance of the selection date, on a Cotton Bowl trip for the Eagles. Every time Miami went ahead, Brock swallowed another inch or so of his cigar. When Flutie came through, it was almost invisible. Luckily, it wasn't lit.

Flutie's heroics should have come as no surprise. In one game, opponent unknown, B.C. trailed by a point in the waning moments, and the opposition was driving.

Flutie told Coach Jack Bicknell, "Coach, we've got to let them score." Bicknell was dumbfounded. Flutie explained that B.C. probably would never see the ball again, but if the opponent scored, they would kick the extra point for an eight-point lead and Flutie could manage to salvage a tie with a touchdown and two-point conversion.

Finally, there was—believe it or not—the Harvard-Yale game of November 23, 1968. You may snicker at Ivy League football, but these were among the best teams in the history of the Ancient Eight. Although both teams were 8-0, unbeaten and untied for the first time since 1909, the two biggest football names were on the Yale side—halfback Calvin Hill, the NFL's Rookie of the Year in 1969, and quarterback Brian Dowling, who hadn't lost a game since the seventh grade and would become the legendary B.D. in a campus comic strip now known as *Doonesbury*. Harvard had career rushing leader Vic Gatto and guard Tommy Lee Jones, of Hollywood fame.

Yale led 22-0 midway through the second quarter. Shortly before halftime, Harvard coach John Yovicsin replaced quarterback George Lalich with backup Frank Champi. Lalich returned to start the second half (It was 22-6 after Champi directed a 64-yard drive) but Harvard couldn't move, and Champi took over again early in the third period.

Three plays later it was 22-13, but Yale scored four minutes into the final period for a 29-13 lead. It remained that way until the final, fateful minute.

With 3 1/2 minutes remaining, Yale's Bob Levin fumbled at the Harvard 14. The Elis never touched the ball again. Champi threw an eight-yard touchdown pass to split end Bruce Freeman with 42 seconds left, and Gus Crim's two-point conversion run made it 29-21.

Naturally, Harvard tried an onside kick—and Bill Kelly recovered at his 49. The Crimson reached the Yale 8 with enough time for one play. Champi threw to Gatto in the corner of the end zone as time expired. Then, Champi hit tight end Pete Varney just inside the goal line for two more points and, as the student newspaper headlined it, "HARVARD WINS, 29-29."

Irony of ironies: Varney played parts of four seasons in the major leagues, and I saw him get his first big-league hit with the Chicago White Sox in 1974. And Champi, a junior, never played another football game.

Down and Dirty

You may wonder why Gene Stallings doesn't wear the Super Bowl ring he earned as an assistant coach with the Dallas Cowboys.

The reason is that it belongs to a corpse.

Jim Fuller, a coach on Stallings' staff at Alabama, told me the story:

"There was this guy from Collinsville, Alabama. He came into Stallings' office and it was a real weird relationship 'cause this guy just came in out of the blue to say hello, whatever, just one of those Alabama fans. They let everybody in. Gene had an open-door policy and anybody that would stop by . . .

"They struck up a conversation and I believe that Gene said, 'Are you going to the ball game?' And the response was, 'No, I ain't going to the game; I ain't got no tickets.'

"Gene said, 'Well, would you go if I give you some?' So he gave him some tickets and the guy kept coming around and introduced himself to us and we all became friends with him. We knew if the boss liked him, we liked him. We'd go on a hunting trip every now and then up to the Tennessee Valley, where Collinsville is.

"He was in there one day and was admiring Coach's ring. Gene said, 'I'll just give you one.' He gave him his pick. Did he want a national championship ring (Alabama in 1992) or the Super Bowl ring. He said, 'I'll take the Super Bowl ring.' Gene was wearing it at the time.

"Then the guy dies. Stallings spoke at his funeral and several of us went up there. The guy's brother, nobody liked him, wanted to get the ring. He [the deceased] was gone, couldn't put it to no use. Stallings said, 'Hey, man, we just gonna bury him with it.' That's what called off the hounds."

And that's the story of Gene Stallings' Super Bowl ring.

Hook 'Em Horns

My first contact with Darrell Royal, the great Texas coach, came in November 1970. My phone rang at home and a voice said, "This is Darrell Royal at the University of Texas."

I figured it was one of my buddies playing a gag. I went along with it and the voice said, "I understand you're handling the All-America team. We've got two mighty fine football players here."

My smart-ass nature got the best of me and I said, "Since you're the number one team in the nation I hope you've got more than two."

Royal explained he was talking about fullback Steve Worster and defensive end Bill Atessis. Since Denne Freeman, the AP man in Dallas, had recommended those two a few days earlier, I knew it was really Royal.

Mack Brown and Darrell Royal (University of Texas)

We chatted for a while and I mentioned my interest in country music, one of Royal's "vices" as well.

A month later I was in Dallas for the second Texas-Notre Dame Cotton Bowl. At one of the press conferences, the rival coaches were asked about strategy for the upcoming game.

Notre Dame's Ara Parseghian went to the blackboard and began diagramming X's and O's ad nauseam. Royal's remarks were shorter and more to the point.

"I reckon we're gonna dance with who brung us," he drawled.

You could see Parseghian sag, and you knew he was thinking, "Why can't I say things like that?"

By the way, you pronounce Ara's name Par-seeg-ian, not Par-seej-ian. Or, as Ara, used to say, "It's par, as in golf; seeg as in Seagram's whiskey, and yen, as in Japanese money. Just think of me as a drunken Japanese golfer."

Notre Dame practiced for the game with 13 men on defense so it would be hard to detect the mirror defense Parseghian was putting up to counter Texas' wishbone look.

During one practice, an AP technician was installing a teletype machine in the press box. Parseghian sent a team manager up to instruct him not to look at the field.

A few nights before the Cotton Bowl, I was sitting in the hospitality suite at the Holiday Inn in Dallas, a few blocks from where John F. Kennedy was shot. Jones Ramsey, the University of Texas sports information director, had just introduced me to nachos without bothering to explain about jalapeño peppers.

I had just downed a few pitchers of ice water to put out the fire when the phone rang. It was Darrell Royal. He told me to grab my guitar and mosey on up to the Texas team hotel. I told him I didn't have wheels and he said he would send someone to pick me up in a blue Buick.

Sure enough, a few minutes later a blue Buick pulled into the driveway.

"Let's go," I said.

"Who're you?" the driver said.

"Didn't Darrell send you?" I asked.

"Darrell who?"

"Darrell Royal," I said.

"I know a Fred Royal in Amarillo," the man said. "Don't know no Darrell Royal."

While this repartee was going on, over the man's shoulder I spotted another blue Buick, the right one. We headed up to the Hilton Hotel on Dallas' Central Expressway, where I serenaded Darrell, his wife, Edith, and the team chaplain, Father Bomar, until the wee hours.

Texas played Auburn in the 1974 Gator Bowl and the teams practiced at Fletcher Junior High School in Jacksonville Beach.

One afternoon, I was sitting in a car alongside the practice field interviewing Auburn coach Shug Jordan when Darrell Royal walked up. I rolled the window down.

"Have you got your axe with you?" he asked (in Royalese, an axe is a guitar).

"It's in the trunk," I said.

"Charley Pride just came into town," Darrell said, "and he'd like to sing for the team, but he hasn't got his axe with him. Can you bring your axe over to the hotel in an hour or so?"

I said sure and Darrell walked away. Shug looked at me and asked, "What does Darrell want with an axe?"

Obviously, he didn't understand Royalese.

Darrell Royal (SPI Archives)

That night, Darrell and Edith Royal, Charley Pride, me and Mr. and Mrs. Paul Davis (Paul, like Darrell, was a former head coach at Mississippi State) made the rounds of what seemed like every watering hole in Jacksonville Beach. At each stop, Darrell introduced Charley Pride, who belted out a song or two. Quite a number of free concerts.

Anchors Aweigh

The U.S. Naval Academy hasn't beaten Notre Dame since 1963 when the Midshipmen had Roger Staubach at the controls. But there was a time when the Irish were torpedoed by another bunch of sailors.

It was a headline you probably will never see again, plastered across all eight columns of the *New York Times* lead sports page on November 28, 1943:

"GR. LAKES TOPS NOTRE DAME, 19-14, IN LAST MINUTE"

It was, of course, the middle of World War II. In October, at the request of Baseball Commissioner Kenesaw Mountain Landis, the Seventh Service Command granted Murry Dickson of the St. Louis Cardinals a 10-day furlough to pitch in the World Series against the New York Yankees (He appeared in the fourth and fifth games, pitching two-thirds of an inning each time). But the War Department, citing mounting transportation needs of the armed forces, canceled a tour of two all-star baseball teams through the South Pacific.

And for two seasons, 1943 and 1944, you could regularly find service teams in the Associated Press college football poll. Not just the service academies, but real military bases, each of which fielded its own team in those truculent times, teams that included college and professional stars.

For example, Charlie Justice, just out of high school in Asheville, North Carolina, was an immediate sensation, helping Bainbridge Naval Training Station to undefeated seasons in 1943 and 1944.

It was at Bainbridge that Justice got his nickname. An observer commented while watching him play, "Say, that Justice kid runs like a choo choo train." The tag stuck and Charlie Justice became Choo Choo Justice, spending two seasons at Bainbridge before being shipped to Hawaii, where he played for the Pearl Harbor Navy All-Stars. When he finally got to the University of North Carolina, Justice set a school total offense record.

Felix "Doc" Blanchard, the great Army fullback who won the 1945 Heisman Trophy, actually began his college football career at North Carolina. He enrolled in 1941, but because of the war the Army took him away and sent him to West Point, where he became a three-time All-American and part of the famed Mr. Inside-Mr. Outside tandem with Glenn Davis.

Blanchard, Davis, Blaik (U.S. Military Academy)

Blanchard had nothing on Barney Poole, who lettered at Mississippi in 1942, at West Point in 1944-45-46 and again at Ole Miss in 1947 and 1948.

By the way, when Justice signed up to enlist in World War II, he was asked which branch of the service he preferred. He told the draft board that since he couldn't swim, he should be in the Army. Justice, of course, was immediately put in the Navy.

Despite its unbeaten records, Bainbridge never got higher than 17th in any of the 1943 polls or fifth in 1944. Other service teams did, although none ever claimed the No. 1 ranking. But the Iowa Pre-Flight Seahawks finished second in 1943, and Randolph Field was third in 1944. North Carolina Pre-Flight also got as high as second in one 1944 poll.

Surely you remember the likes of March Field, Del Monte Pre-Flight and Fourth Air Force. All appeared in the Top Ten. And don't forget Memphis Naval, Camp Grant, the San Diego Naval Zoomers, the Second Air Force Superbombers, Third Air Force, Norman Naval (Didn't you know Oklahoma is on an ocean?), El Toro Marines, Camp Peary, Fort Pierce and St. Mary's Naval Pre-Flight, featuring Minnesota's 1941 Heisman Trophy winner Bruce Smith. All fielded Top Twenty teams.

Randolph Field, with Tulsa All-American Glenn Dobbs, tied Texas 7-7 in the January 1, 1944, Cotton Bowl, and the Second Air Force beat Hardin-Simmons 13-7 in the 1943 Sun Bowl.

The Great Lakes Bluejackets only wound up sixth after beating national champion Notre Dame in 1943, the only blemish on the Irish's 9-1 campaign (a good wartime word, don't you think?). And this was a Notre Dame team with Johnny Lujack at quarterback, Ziggy Czarobski at tackle and John Yonakor at end.

Miracles routinely occur at Notre Dame, and this game produced two, one for the Irish and one against them. The first was a last-minute, 46-yard Great Lakes pass for the winning touchdown. It was thrown by Steve Lach, a former Duke and Chicago Cardinals star, and caught by one Paul Anderson. The second miracle was the final AP poll two days later, which made Notre Dame the only team ever to be voted national champion after losing its final game.

(Before any Minnesota fans start howling, the Golden Gophers won the 1960 crown but lost their bowl game *after* the final poll, which was taken *before* the bowls in those days.)

Ironically, one of the Great Lakes stars was Emil "Six Yard" Sitko, who joined the Navy as a Notre Dame freshman and later starred for the Irish after the war, lettering four times. Sitko scored the sailors' first touchdown on a 16-yard run. For the record, Great Lakes that year also beat Pitt 40-0 and Ohio State 13-6.

A few weeks before defeating Notre Dame, Great Lakes, aided by Lt. Bill Osmanski, a former Chicago Bears star, joined the growing list of teams employing the T-formation.

In 1943, Southwestern University, bolstered by former Texas stars transplanted under a Marine training program, beat the Longhorns 14-7.

Led by Wisconsin's Pat Harder and Fordham's Steve Filipowicz, both of whom went on to NFL stardom, the Georgia Pre-Flight Skycrackers crushed Newberry College 53-0, with the last two periods trimmed from 15 to 10 minutes by mutual agreement.

Shortly after a surprising 10-6 upset of Temple, little Ursinus College of Collegeville, Pennsylvania, canceled its last game of 1943 when Coach Pete Stevens was accepted for Army induction and a number of players were called to active military service.

The 1943 University of Pennsylvania team had nine starters who were Navy trainees under the V-5 and V-12 programs. On the other hand, seven Wisconsin players were transferred to the Iowa Naval Pre-Flight School in Iowa City under the V-5 program.

Otto Graham, who led Northwestern in total offense and passing in 1941, 1942 and 1943 and later starred for the Cleveland Browns, played for the 1944 North Carolina Pre-Flight Cloudbusters.

They don't make nicknames—or teams—like those anymore. Hopefully, they never will again.

By the way, despite Notre Dame's dominance of Navy, the Rev. Theodore Hesburgh, former president of Notre Dame, always credited the Navy Department with keeping Notre Dame's doors open during the war by assigning scores of Naval recruits to the South Bend school.

On, Brave Old Army Team

The quote is featured prominently in every West Point football guide. It was uttered by Gen. George C. Marshall, the U.S. Army's chief of staff during World War II: "I want an officer for a secret and dangerous mission. I want a West Point football player."

When Tom Cahill was Army's head coach in the early 1970s, he came down to New York City every week to attend the weekly luncheon of the New York Football Writers Association.

One week, the subject of golf came up. Said Cahill, "Show me a coach who spends all his time on the golf course; I want him on my schedule."

"Okay," said Gordon White of the *New York Times*, "would you rather open with Darrell Royal or Chuck Fairbanks?"

Cahill learned the hard way that not every West Pointer followed orders to the letter. He once sent a player into a game with instructions to tell the quarterback to run the next play on a long count.

Guess who jumped offside on the first "hut"? Right, the messenger.

Army and Cahill caught a lot of flak for losing the 1972 opener to Nebraska 77-7. What people didn't realize was that (1) Nebraska wasn't a national power when the game was scheduled, but was coming off two straight national championships, (2) the Cornhuskers could only travel with 50 players under Big Eight rules and (3) Army turned the ball over five times inside its 20-yard line.

Nevertheless, Cahill received a telegram from a retired general complaining that "if this is the type of young men West Point is turning out these days I'm going to buy Russian war bonds."

In 1971, Army's quarterback was J. Kingsley Fink. In late October, the Cadets traveled to Miami, blew a halftime lead and lost to the Hurricanes 24-13, a game Cahill felt they should have won.

Arrangements had been made for Cahill to talk to the media after the game for a set period of time. That period had expired and Cahill was just emerging from the shower when along came a young reporter from the *Miami Herald.*

"Sorry," snapped Cahill, who wasn't in the best of moods anyway, "I've already talked to the press."

The young fellow explained that he was on deadline when the game ended and couldn't get downstairs in time to hear Cahill's remarks.

"All right," Cahill finally said, "what do you want to know?"

"What did you tell your team at halftime?" the young fellow asked.

"There are three things I never discuss," Cahill said somewhat testily—"my wife's age, how much money I make and what I tell my team at halftime."

A few more questions elicited the same kind of snappish answers.

The lead paragraph in the next day's paper read, "There's more than one Fink on the Army football team."

When Army added an upper deck to the west side of Michie Stadium (pronounced Mikey) in 1969, it provided a roof, but no windows in the event of inclement weather.

They lucked out until 1972, when a couple of games were played in torrential rains which slanted into the press box. There are only two rows of seats, the front one for the print media and the rear one for broadcasters, statisticians, etc.

In those days, we still used typewriters, but it rained so hard that you couldn't sit in the front row without getting soaked, so we had to huddle against the rear wall. I never opened my typewriter, just dictated my game story off the top of my head.

As president of the New York Football Writers that year, I wrote to the superintendent of the Military Academy explaining the problem.

My opening line went something like this: "Far be it from me to tell an Army man about field conditions, but this is ridiculous."

I received a note back agreeing with my assessment and telling me the project had been turned over to the Army Corps of Engineers. That's when I suspected we were really in the deep stuff. Army opened the 1973 season on the most gorgeous day one could want—warm and sunny. There was no need for windows and there weren't any, but the window frames were in place.

I got hold of sports information director Bob Kinney and gave him a quizzical look.

"I'll tell you," he said, "but you can't write it."

You should know that there is no press elevator at Michie Stadium, where you have to trudge up through the stands and the press box is situated right up there with Mount Everest.

Seems the Army Corps of Engineers had lugged the window glass up the previous day only to find it was half an inch too small for the frames.

However, the next week the glass was in place and that's why the Michie Stadium press box has windows.

A couple of days after Army lost to Navy 28-0 to wind up a 4-6-1 1978 season, I received a call at work from Homer Smith, who had just been dismissed as coach of the Cadets.

"Can you come up here tomorrow?" he asked.

I said that I had to work the following day.

"Can I come down there?" he asked.

I suspected something was up. At the appointed hour, Homer came in and we adjourned to the AP's Pto-maine Palace (i.e., cafeteria) for a cup of coffee. Homer handed me a sheaf of papers. As I read them, I realized he was accusing the United States Military Academy of numerous NCAA violations. There were no cars and no buying of players, mostly violations of the sort coaches would call "chicken-shit," but violations nonetheless.

It wasn't the best of times for Homer, who was bitter over his firing and whose brother had been killed a few weeks earlier when a train smashed into his car. I gave him several chances to back out. He didn't.

I called my sports editor at home. He told me to write the story but to leave it in the computer system overnight so the AP lawyers could check it out.

The next afternoon, an advisory moved on the sports wire that within the hour we would move a story charging one of the nation's most prominent football programs with the violations. A friend of mine at one of the Detroit papers said his sports staff took a pool as to which school was involved. No one won because no one guessed Army. Oklahoma was a popular choice.

By the way, every college football fan should attend a game at West Point in late October-early November when the leaves are changing colors. There may not be a better venue in college football at that time of year. And be sure not to miss the 10 a.m. parade of Cadets on the Plain.

Army opened the 1975 season, Homer Smith's second as head coach, by ripping Holy Cross 44-7. At the postgame press conference, Smith was asked if this meant Army was becoming a football dynasty again.

Smith pointed out that his players, like all the West Point cadets, had to rise for 6 a.m. reveille, march in formation, eat breakfast with the rest of the corps, etc.

"If that's a dynasty, then I guess that's what we are," Smith said.

Things have changed since, and the Army team is now allowed to go offcampus the night before a home game.

Alabama-Auburn may be the bitterest rivalry in college football, but there's nothing like Army-Navy to make you feel proud and patriotic when the Corps of Cadets and Brigade of Midshipmen parade into the stadium a few hours before the kickoff.

Whoever the president was attended one game when it was still played at old John F. Kennedy (nee Municipal) Stadium in Philadelphia before Veterans Stadium was built across the street.

Wherever the president goes, the Secret Service is sure to follow. Also, to precede.

I got to the stadium about two-and-a-half hours before game time and a Secret Service agent was standing in the press box at parade rest on the 50-yard line. He never moved during the pregame festivities or the game itself. I'm not even sure if he breathed.

Zebras

There was a split crew of officials for the 1979 Tennessee-Boston College game in Chestnut Hill, Massachusetts. The referee was Jim Garvey, the top referee in the East for a number of years. One of his pet peeves was split crews.

"I always felt they really are 'our guys' and 'your guys,'" Garvey says.

In that Tennessee-BC game, the umpire and two wing officials came from the other Southeastern Conference.

"In our pregame, we did our usual story when we talk about everybody being on the up-and-up, and let's make sure that every foul is in the film, and so on and so forth," Garvey remembers.

"As you might imagine, we had five major fouls in the first half called by basically the umpire and the two [SEC] wing officials, all against Boston College. And as we're leaving the field at halftime (Boston College coach Ed) Chlebek runs up to me.

"I can't believe that not one foul was called . . . when are we gonna get a foul, pass interference, called our way?" Chlebek sputtered.

Garvey couldn't resist. "I said, 'Coach, as soon as you figure out where our [Eastern] officials line up and throw the ball on that side of the field.'

"He looked and me and said, 'Thanks.'"

"I'll tell you how that game began, which is what makes this story kind of amusing.

"It was a night game, and the coach of Tennessee was none other than John Majors. And of course we had had him in our group at Pitt for many, many years.

"So prior to the game, an hour and a half before the game, the umpire and the referee visit each coach. So I go in with this umpire from the Southeastern Conference, who shall remain nameless, and in just trying to make conversation, this umpire says to Coach Majors, 'Did you hear any scores this afternoon?'

John Majors (University of Pittsburgh)

"And Majors reports back, 'Well, Notre Dame beat somebody by this score and Army I think beat . . .'

"And he goes, 'Coach, I don't care about those scores. How did OUR boys do?' And Majors told him that Auburn had beaten someone and Ole Miss, and he gave the Southeastern Conference results, and not to be outdone, having known John Majors for maybe 10 years, and officiated for him, I said, 'Coach, it's nice to see you. By the way, how did OUR boys do this afternoon?'

"And as soon as I said that, the umpire knew he'd made a big mistake.

"I hated that stuff, our guys and your guys. I always had a feeling in split crew games that these kinds of things were bound to happen."

Jim Garvey remembers a Boston College-Clemson game.

"[Doug] Flutie was playing William 'The Refrigerator' Perry, and it was a heck of a good game. And for three periods, William the Refrigerator was every bit as quick as Flutie and we couldn't catch him. It was like a bear chasing a rabbit.

"But as the night wore on, it was a hot September night, William tired and Flutie brought his team back to the point where Boston College was one extra point from tying the game. And we had an offside by the defensive team, Clemson, which led us to an interesting type of a decision.

"Boston College could have accepted the penalty and kicked an extra point for the tie and had the five yards assessed on the kickoff, or they could have had a half-the-distance-to-the-goal penalty and moved the ball down to the one and a half and maybe go for two.

"Normally when there's a decision that doesn't involve much thought, sometimes the referee would make the decision and move on to keep the game moving. But this was one that I thought I wanted Flutie to understand.

"Jack Bicknell's assistant at the time is a good friend of mine and now is the head coach at Northeastern. Barry was standing next to Jack, and Barry didn't even allow me to give the explanation. He wanted to keep the point and let's go.

"But Jack wasn't sure, and Flutie being the only calm guy in the whole ballpark, including myself, I was trying to give the explanation, he was trying to listen, and the two coaches for Boston College were animated as we were doing this.

"Flutie finally took charge of the whole situation and in kind of a crisp tone said, 'Will everybody please shut up and let him talk plain to me. He's the only one here who knows what's going on.'

"And all the coaches immediately froze, but that's kind of the way Flutie was."

"Temple is playing East Carolina, and East Carolina had a punt returner named Henry Williams. He went on to the National Football League, and every time he scored he did a back flip in the end zone.

"Early in the game there's a punt to Temple and Temple runs the ball back for a touchdown, but we had an official named Walt Malinchak, he was from Monesson, Pennsylvania, and he was a funny guy with a big chaw of tobacco. He was a railroad man and he throws a flag for clipping, so the Temple touchdown comes back.

"It was a very close game. Second half, same situation reversed, punting to East Carolina, and Henry Williams catches the kick and he jitterbugs and he dances, he kinda shucks and jives, he's got people from all different angles, and I see Malinchak's flag go in there and this guy breaks loose and he goes about 80 yards for a touchdown.

"I don't put my hands up 'cause I've seen the flag. Al Benson is the linesman on that side. He comes running up and he says to me, 'You better go talk to [Temple coach Bruce] Arians; he's gonna go crazy.'

"I said, 'No problem, we got a clip back there. I saw Malinchak's flag.' He said, 'Look again.' So I looked up and I don't see any flags. So I said, 'What happened?' He says, 'Malinchak threw the flag, but as the guy broke into the clear, he ran over, picked up the flag and put it back in his pocket.'

"I said, 'What! He can't do that.' He said, 'He did it.' And Arians is going crazy. Henry Williams is doing back flips in the end zone, he's just scored the winning touchdown and in my mind I'm saying, 'Well, that's sorta fair; they've [Temple] lost one, now they've (East Carolina) lost one, it kinda washes.' But no, he ran over, picked up the flag and put it in his pocket.

"There was just no way to tell a coach how that could be. I said, 'Coach, you're gonna be very displeased with the decision that our crew has made, but the official believed that he made a mistake and he tried to rectify it.'

"All he [Arians] told me was that when he looked at his films that call better be right. I said the same thing. Malinchak didn't stay in the league very long."

"Probably the cutest story I ever had was an off-the-field story that occurred with a guy named Wayne Hardin. Wayne coached at Navy and was coaching at Temple when this occurred.

"I was a young official invited to address the entire, what is now the Big East Conference, but at that time it was all the major Eastern independents up at Cape Cod with the bowl officials on the new rules. And in the audience was Joe Paterno and the coach from Syracuse, Dick MacPherson, and people of that type. Jim Young was the coach at Army, so these were quite a good group of coaches and I was a young referee.

"And I gave my presentation on the new rules for the year and everybody was quite respectful. I asked were there any questions. And the curmudgeon in the back, Wayne Hardin, puts his hand up and he says, 'Young fellow, for the last 10 years we've been screwed by Penn

State because when we get down near the goal line and we line up our flanker, we just have our quarterback throw the ball up in the air on a fade route because we know that they're gonna smack our receiver, and you've just gotten through telling us that when the ball's in the air, the defensive people cannot make contact with that receiver. Isn't that true?'

"Now I'm standing up there at the microphone and I'm saying, 'Holy Jesus, what he says does make some sense, but how am I gonna answer this question? It's really not a question, it's a statement.' And as I thought about it, I realized for the first time that I was assigned in the upcoming season to the Penn State-Temple game in Veterans Stadium.

"So trying to make some humor out of it, a little tense situation, I said, 'Coach, that's a very good question and I'll answer it this way. For the first time, I'm assigned that game, and in all likelihood I will observe you being screwed for the 11th time when that guy breaks off the line and the ball is thrown, because if it happens real quick, the likelihood is no flag will be thrown.

"And everybody laughed, including Hardin, and we got away with a tough situation."

My Namesake

Believe it or not, Herschel Walker and I were both named after our grandfathers. No, we didn't have the same grandfather, in case you were wondering.

I first met Herschel Walker in 1979 when he was a senior at Wrightsville (Georgia) High School. He came to New York as part of a deal in which the Hertz Corp. named the outstanding high school athlete from each state.

I introduced myself and told him, "Don't disgrace the name."

He didn't. But he did misspell it; at least he misspelled my name when he sent me an autographed picture. Since we both spell our names the same way, I've got to think he did it intentionally.

Herschel Walker and I rode in the same elevator at a banquet in New Haven, Connecticut, one year and someone said it might be the first time two Herschels were on one elevator.

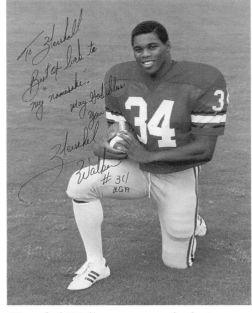

Herschel Walker autographed picture
(Photo courtesy of Herschel Nissenson)

183

"Yeah," Herschel Walker said, "but only one's good-looking."

I don't think he was referring to me.

I went to Dallas one year to interview Eric Dickerson, the great SMU running back. As Dickerson entered the room, Bob Condron, the SMU sports information director, introduced us, saying, "Eric, I'd like you to meet Herschel Walker."

"Gee," Dickerson said without batting an eyelash, "I'd thought you'd be bigger."

Why Some Prospects Don't Make Their SAT Score

Everyone's heard of the recruit who filled out a questionnaire, and in the space for "Church Preference" wrote "Red Brick." Or for "Sex" answered, "One night in Laredo."

Rice University, of all schools, once recruited a prospect who listed his vertical jump as 32 inches, or whatever. The next line asked "SAT." "No," the prospect wrote, "I was standing."

But not all players have the IQ of an uninflated football. So it was that when Dartmouth was looking for a head coach following the 1977 season, I received a phone call from Larry Lacewell, then the defensive coordinator at Oklahoma.

"Do you know anyone at Dartmouth?" he asked. "Can you put my hat in the ring?"

I knew the athletic director pretty well, but I asked Lacewell, "Why on earth do you want to coach in the Ivy League?"

"Before my career is over," he said, "my ambition is to coach a team where I'd only have to tell the players what to do one time."

Some of the answers players put down in their questionnaires are classics.

There was an Arkansas player in the 1970s who, on the line for "Father's Alma Mater," wrote, "A winner never quits, a quitter never wins."

And a Rice recruit once returned a summer school dorm key with a letter that began, "Dear College."

The Bowl Championship Series, Alias the Bowl Crime Syndicate

I once flunked a math course in college. When I repeated the class, I wound up with the same professor, who asked me, "Are you making a career of my course?"

Thank goodness the course wasn't that taught by Prof. Roy Kramer and his colleagues in the Bowl Crime Syndicate—sorry, the Bowl Championship Series.

In 1999, Kramer & Co. did some tweaking to the selection process that sends the nation's 1-2 teams to the national championship game. Here's the remedial version:

"Any Division I-A team can qualify for selection in the BCS if they have won at least nine college football games during the most recently completed regular season (not to include wins in exempted games) and are ranked in the top 12 of the final BCS standings." Exempted games are the Kickoff Classic, Pigskin Classic, etc.

Let's go to the advanced course:

"The rating system will consist of the same four major components used in 1998: subjective polls of the writers and coaches, computer rankings, schedule strength and number of losses. The two teams which have the lowest point total in the four categories will play in the national championship game."

Polls: "The poll component will be calculated based on the average of the ranking of each team in the Associated Press media poll and the *USA Today*/ESPN coaches poll. The rankings of each team will be added and divided by two. For example, a team ranked number one in one poll and number two in the other poll would receive 1.5 points in this component (1+2=3/2=1.5)."

Computer Rankings: "The second component will consist of eight computer rankings. These computer rankings will include the three used last year (*New York Times*, Jeff Sagarin's *USA Today* and the Anderson-Hester *Seattle Times*) along with five additional rankings (Richard Billingsley, Dunkel Index, Kenneth Massey, David Rothman and the Matthews/Scripps-Howard rankings). The computer component will be determined by averaging the seven highest computer rankings. The lowest computer ranking will be disregarded. For example, if a team is ranked first in four polls, second in three polls and third in another, the ranking in which the team is third will be disregarded and the remaining seven polls will be added and divided by seven (1, 1, 1, 1, 2, 2, 2=10/7=1.43)."

Strength of Schedule: "The third component will be the team's strength of schedule. This component is calculated by determining the cumulative won/lost records of the team's opponents and the cumulative won/loss records of the team's opponents' opponents. The formula shall be weighted two-thirds (66 2/3 percent) for the opponents' record and one third (33 1/3 percent) for the opponents' opponents' record. The team's schedule strength shall be calculated to determine in which quartile it will rank—1-25, 26-50, 51-75, 76-100—and shall be further quantified by its ranking within each quartile (divided by 25). For example, if a team's schedule strength rating is 28th in the nation, that team would receive 1.12 points (28/25=1.12). Should a team play a Division I-AA opponent, only the losses of the Division I-AA team shall be used in determining the opponents' record or the opponents' opponents' record."

Losses: "Each loss during the season will represent one point in this component.

"All four components shall be added together for a total rating. The team with the lowest point total shall rank first in the Bowl Championship standings."

Remember, this formula is used only to determine the championship game. There is nothing to prevent a repeat of what happened to Kansas State in 1998 and again in 1999 when the Wildcats were shut out of the BCS bowls.

One final thought: Before Einstein, it was known that a beam of light pushes against matter; this is known as radiation pressure. This means the light has momentum. A beam of light Energy (E) has momentum E/c. Einstein used this fact to show that radiation (light) energy has an equivalent mass.

Picture, if you will, a cylinder of mass (M). A pulse of light with energy (E) is emitted from the left side. The cylinder recoils to the left with velocity $[v=E/(Mc)]$. If the mass of the cylinder is large, it doesn't move far before the light reaches the other side. So the light must travel a distance (L), requiring time $(t=L/c)$. In this time, the cylinder travels a distance $[x=vt=[E/(Mc)](L/c)]$.

Congratulations. You now know the theory of relativity. Would that the BCS formula were as simple.

The Bitterest Rivalry of Them All

David Housel is the athletic director at Auburn University. Housel grew up in Gordo, Alabama, a few miles west of Tuscaloosa, but he is an Auburn man through and through. He bleeds orange and blue—and I wouldn't be surprised if that were literally true.

Back when he was Auburn's sports information director, I once posed two scenarios and asked him to choose one:

1. Auburn could go 11-1 and win the national championship, but the loss would be to Alabama.

2. Auburn could go 1-10, but the victory would come against Alabama.

Pat Dye, David Housel, Bo Jackson, Herschel Nissenson with the Heisman Trophy (Photo courtesy of Herschel Nissenson)

190

Housel had no hesitation in picking No. 2.

You've probably heard that the Alabama-Auburn rivalry makes every other rivalry appear tame. Believe it. And more so off the field than on it.

I know some folks in the same office in the Jefferson County Department of Revenue in Birmingham. One's computer screen continuously scrolls "Roll Tide," the other's keeps repeating "War Eagle," Auburn's battle cry.

I once knew a fellow from an Auburn family who was the first member of his family to attend Alabama. His father didn't speak to him for three years. Really.

Alabama-Auburn is more than a once-a-year happening. If your team loses, you suffer for 365 days . . . or until your side wins.

Alabama-Auburn affects more families than any other rivalry. Husbands and wives, parents and children.

The rivalry began on Feb. 22, 1893, at Birmingham's Lakeview Park. Auburn won 32-22. After the 1907 game, the schools argued over expenses and officiating. They couldn't agree on how much money each player should be allotted for the annual trip to Birmingham. Auburn wanted $3.50 a day, Alabama countered with $3.00. In addition, Auburn wanted a Northern official, Alabama held out for a Southerner.

That seemingly minor quarrel turned into a 41-year break in the series. In 1923, Auburn president Dr. Spright Dowell said the game should not be played because "football would tend to become the all-time topic of both institutions." In 1944, Alabama's Board of Trustees said a resumption would "result in an accelerated overemphasis of football in the state." Little did they know.

It took a resolution by the Alabama House of Representatives to jump-start the rivalry. On December 4, 1948, Alabama won 55-0 at Birmingham's Legion Field, the game's annual home until 1989, when Auburn decided to play at its Jordan-Hare Stadium when it was the home team. Alabama countered by moving its home games with Auburn to Tuscaloosa.

In the 25 years that Bear Bryant coached at Alabama, Auburn deluded itself into thinking it was Bama's arch-rival. The Bear insisted the game was simply for bragging rights. Actually, he liked nothing better than beating Tennessee, a school against which he was 1-5-2 during his years at Kentucky and was shut out five times.

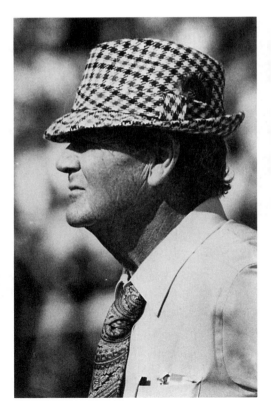

The Bear inflamed passions shortly before the 1972 contest when he said he would rather "beat that cow college once than beat Texas 10 times."

And one morning when Bryant called Auburn around 7 a.m., only to find that Coach

Bear Bryant
(SPI Archives)

Shug Jordan wasn't in yet, he needled the secretary, "Don't you people take football seriously down there?"

The folks at Auburn had a good laugh when Alabama hired Bill Curry as its head coach in 1987.

There are two things you don't do at Alabama—hire a coach with a losing record or a coach with ties to Auburn, Tennessee or Georgia Tech. Alabama president Joab Thomas did both—Curry had a record of 31-43-4 at Georgia Tech and was a former Georgia Tech star, to boot.

I happened to be talking with a member of the Auburn athletic department about a month after Curry's hiring and he was still chuckling.

Bill Curry (Georgia Tech)

"You know," I said, "Curry didn't really have a chance to win at Georgia Tech."

"Even at Georgia Tech," came the reply, "they expect you to beat Furman."

I looked it up; Curry was 0-1-1 against Furman.

Hang Down Your Head, Vince Dooley

During the 1980 season, Barbara Dooley mentioned to husband Vince, then Georgia's head coach, that her mother, a well-known hostess at a Birmingham, Alabama, restaurant, had called asking about the Georgia team and its upcoming opponent for four or five straight weeks.

"I think your mother's betting on the games," Vince reasoned.

Vince Dooley (University of Georgia)

Sure enough she was, giving the points when Georgia was favored and taking the points when the Bulldogs were underdawgs.

"How can you enjoy a football game without a bet on it?" Barbara's mother explained when her daughter asked her about it.

In the regular-season finale, Georgia, en route to a national championship behind Herschel Walker, was an 18 1/2-point favorite over Georgia Tech.

Midway through the fourth quarter, Georgia led 38-20. That's 18 points, not 18 1/2.

With 7:17 left to play, Georgia took over on downs at the Tech 47. Nine plays later—seven rushes, one incomplete pass and a run for no gain on third-and-eight at the Tech 13, well within field-goal range—Georgia gave the ball back with 4:03 remaining.

The Dawgs had one last chance to cover the spread when Tommy Thurson intercepted a Tech pass at the Georgia 35 with 1:42 left. Six running plays, plus a personal foul against Tech, moved the ball to the Yellow Jackets 20, again in field goal range.

A running play lost a yard and time expired, leaving Georgia with a 38-20 win and Barbara Dooley's mother out $25.

"When we went home for Christmas, she gave Vince hell for not kicking a field goal," Barbara recalls.

Barbara Dooley's mother apparently never heard the best gambling story of all time, which may have cured her of betting on football games.

There is no evidence that anyone bet on the Rutgers-Princeton contest in 1869 that kicked off the sport of football. There also is no evidence that anyone didn't, either. Wagering on football probably has been going on since they played without helmets (the players, not the bettors).

There are plenty of way to lose a bet, but probably none stranger than that which befell some Vanderbilt—Vanderbilt?—players in 1969. The story has been making the rounds for years and has been embellished somewhat to include a $3,000 bet and a year and a half to pay off the losses.

Nothing like that, says Pat Toomay, a Vanderbilt end who later starred for the Dallas Cowboys and concedes he may have done some of the embellishing. Toomay recounts the story in his book *The Crunch*, published in 1975 by W.W. Norton & Co., Inc. It involved the 1969 Vandy-Tulane game in New Orleans, which wasn't exactly Florida-Florida State since both teams came in with 1-5 records. Toomay says it was nothing more than the betting cards one can find most anywhere.

I'll give both versions of the story.

"A couple of days before the game," Toomay writes, "several of Vandy's stalwarts were lolling around Jerry's Pub in Nashville, downing some brew and studying the week's betting line. Vanderbilt was a three-point favorite (Actually it was four).

"'We can beat them sumbitches by more than three,'
Neal Smith announced. He circled Vanderbilt and two
other favorites on the card and plunked down 10 dollars.
Homer, the bartender, took the 10-spot and gave Neal a
copy of his selections.

"'Goddamn, you're right,' John Miller said. 'Give
me one of them sheets, Homer.' Miller made the same
selections and plunked down his life's savings, 25 dollars.
Winning all three games would have tripled Miller's
money.

"Late in the third quarter," Toomay writes, "things
weren't looking too bad. The scores of the other games
were in, and everyone was two-for-two. By the fourth
quarter, however, a major problem had developed; we
were losing our game (Tulane went ahead 21-20 with
2:06 left to play) and time was growing short. In fact, it
was fourth-and-15 . . . with less than two minutes to
play. In a last-ditch effort, Dave Strong went as deep as
possible and Denny Painter threw it as far as he could.
Two Tulane defenders leaped beautifully to make the interception—and missed. Dave scooped the tipped ball
from his shoelaces and scampered the remaining 50 yards
to score (completing a 79-yard play) . . . We were comfortably ahead by four (actually it was 26-21).

"With 30 seconds left in the game (the play-by-play
says 1:04) we got possession of the ball deep in our own
territory again (the aforementioned Neal Smith intercepted a pass at the Vandy 21, but three running plays
lost seven yards, and a delay-of-game penalty pushed the
ball back to the nine). Painter called a time-out.
'MILLER!' It was Coach [Bill] Pace. Miller was the

backup quarterback and Coach Pace carefully instructed him. John sulked back to the bench, the boys gathered round.

"'You're not going to believe this,' John stammered, his voice cracking. 'That son-of-a-bitch wants me to go into the game, take the snap from center, run around for as long as I can and fall in the end zone for a goddamn safety.'"

The safety, of course, would have trimmed Vandy's lead from five points to three; remember, the Commodores were favored by four.

"John replaced Painter at quarterback (The play-by-play says he replaced Watson Brown), did as he was told (Vandy won 26-23) and dropped a veritable fortune."

The play-by-play sheet merely notes, "Miller tackled in the end zone by Young." It does not say why several Vanderbilt players felt they had lost.

The other version goes that Toomay and a few teammates had been betting on games—not Vanderbilt games —with a Nashville bookie for several weeks. They raised every penny they could to bet on the Tulane game. Their girlfriends were hocking their jewelry and they plunked down $3,000 on Vandy. At halftime, having given four points, Vandy was locked in a 13-13 tie. Toomay was trying to fire everyone up in the dressing room, and the Vandy players—remember, only a handful were in on this—looked strangely at one another, wondering why he was so excited about Tulane.

With 1:34 left in the game, having given four points, Vandy went ahead 26-21 on the Painter-to-Strong pass play. Watson Brown, who was not part of the betting ring, remembers that two Tulane defenders tipped the ball.

Vandy then kicked off into the end zone for a touch-back and Tulane completed a 31-yard pass to the Vandy 49. On the next play, however, Vandy's Smith intercepted a pass at the Commodores' 21 with 1:04 left to play. On three keepers, quarterback Brown, who doesn't remember being in the game, lost seven yards, and a delay-of-game penalty pushed the ball back to the Vandy nine.

Vandy called time out and Pace gave Miller his instructions, which enraged Toomay, who reportedly said, "You kneel down in the end zone and I'll break both your legs."

Miller did, Toomay didn't and it took them 19 months to pay off the bookie.

I like the second version better.

Hayden Fry

In announcing his retirement as Iowa's head coach at the end of the 1998 season, Hayden Fry tearfully said he didn't want to coach more games than Bear Bryant or win more Big Ten games than Woody Hayes or Bo Schembechler because "I'm not in their class as a coach."

That's open for discussion, considering the state of Iowa football when Fry took over, but he accomplished something in his career that Bryant, Hayes and Schembechler never did—he took a team to a bowl game with a losing record. It had never happened before—it has happened three times since—and it couldn't happen today, since NCAA rules now say a team must have a winning record to go bowling.

The year was 1963. The team was Southern Methodist University. The Sun Bowl, fourth oldest of all the postseason games behind the Rose, Orange and Sugar Bowls, felt it needed big-name schools to become a major attraction.

Hayden Fry (University of Iowa)

The Sun Bowl had been inviting the likes of Hardin-Simmons, Southwestern (Texas), UTEP and New Mexico State. For example, the January 1, 1943, game matched Hardin-Simmons against the Second Air Force, a service team. Two years later, Southwestern played the University of Mexico (not *New* Mexico).

In 1962, West Texas State defeated Ohio University 15-14. The following year, the Sun Bowl went big-time by inviting 7-3 Oregon and 4-6 SMU, which had tied for sixth place in the Southwest Conference and where Fry was in his second year as head coach. The Sun Bowl took notice of the fact that SMU had defeated a fourth-ranked Navy team 32-28 early in the season. Sun Bowl officials have always credited the SMU-Oregon game with putting it over the hump as a respected player in the bowl business.

In 1979, Fry inherited an Iowa program that hadn't had a winning season since 1961 and had won only 29 games in the 10 previous years. Fry brought Iowa three Big Ten championships, three Rose Bowls and 14 bowl trips. His overall record in 20 years was 143-89-6 and his 37-year mark at SMU (1962-72), North Texas State (1973-78) and Iowa was 232-178-10.

A little-known fact about Fry —one of his pupils at Odessa (Texas) High School was a young man from the nearby community of Wink who was musically inclined and had a band known as the Wink Westerners. The course was Texas history; the young man's name was Roy Orbison.

Grambling Family Robinson

Eddie Robinson remembers his first game as Grambling's head coach, which means he has a good memory because it was played in 1941. The school was known then as the Colored Industrial & Agricultural Institute of Lincoln Parish, Bear Bryant was four years away from becoming a head coach, Joe Paterno and Bobby Bowden were in grade school and Pearl Harbor was a few months off. The opponent was Philander Smith College and the game was played in Little Rock.

Grambling lost, the start of a 3-5 season during which Robinson had to run off some players. The next

Eddie Robinson (Grambling State University)

year, with 33 of the 67 men enrolled in the school on the team, the Tigers not only were unbeaten and untied (9-0), but also were unscored upon, the last team to shut out every opponent.

Robinson lasted 55 seasons, all at Grambling, and retired after the 1996 campaign with a record of 408-165-15. No other coach at any level of college football has approached 400 wins, and only Amos Alonzo Stagg coached longer, 57 years as a head coach, with 94 fewer victories than Robinson.

Robinson coached well into his 70s and lasted so long that his own school—Leland College in suburban Baton Rouge, where he was a star quarterback—no longer exists.

"It's a hell of a thing living in America," Eddie Robinson said in 1995 shortly before his 400th victory.

Life for Robinson wasn't always a rose garden. The living conditions in Grambling, Louisiana, more than half a century ago almost ended his career before it began. He was born in Jackson, Louisiana, son of a sharecropper father and a domestic-worker mother, and raised in Baton Rouge.

After graduating from Leland, Robinson went to work at a feed mill for 25 cents an hour and delivered ice and worked on a coal truck to earn extra income. He heard that a black school some 60 miles east of Shreveport was looking for a football coach and he got the job. He was 22 years old. For $63.75 a month, he also mowed the field, marked the lines, taped ankles, directed the girls' drill squad, drove injured players to the doctor (The NCAA probably would frown on that today), wrote his own press releases and even wrote the game story for the newspapers. He also made sandwiches for road trips because the team couldn't eat in segregated restaurants.

"I really wanted to work in Baton Rouge," Robinson says. "That's as far as I'd been. I thought about working in Baton Rouge at the high school I graduated from. But I really needed a job because we were expecting. I figured I could work for a couple of years and come back to Baton Rouge."

"A couple of years" became 55, during which Robinson had only one serious job offer—the Los Angeles Rams came calling when he was a young pup of 58—and he sent out only one job application, to Southern University in Baton Rouge after the perfect 1942 season.

"In the '40s, Grambling was a rural town, and the only running water was on campus," Robinson explains. "There was well water out in the community. We had to boil the water and the kids got ill. I sent my wife back to Baton Rouge to let the doctors there go over our kids. The living conditions were really tough."

What changed Robinson's mind was a visit to Grambling's remarkable president, Dr. Ralph Waldo Emerson Jones.

"There were apartments on campus and other people were living there," Robinson says. "I didn't feel I was important enough to single me out. I said that [the living conditions] was the only thing making me go. He said, 'I'll determine how important you are. One apartment is free now.' We got that apartment and then in the early '50s he put me off campus and made me build a house."

The Rams came close to getting Robinson after the 1977 season. "Carroll Rosenbloom [the owner] asked me how much I made," Robinson says. "He said, 'You write down how much you make and I'll write down how much I'll pay you.' The offer was out of sight. I never dreamed of making that kind of money. But there was no chance of my leaving a championship team at Grambling. The money was great but I wanted to be there with a championship team."

There were 17 Southwestern Athletic Conference championships and nine national black college crowns. The honors started coming with a Football Writers Association of America citation in 1966 as "The Coach Who Made the Biggest Contribution to College Football in the Past 25 Years." They include the prestigious Bobby Dodd Coach of the Year Award in 1993—the only black, and only Division I-AA, coach so honored—the National Football Foundation & College Hall of Fame Outstanding Contribution to Amateur Football Award (1992), the Independence Bowl's Omar Bradley Spirit of Independence Award (1988) and a Distinguished American citation from the Walter Camp Football Foundation (1982).

At the NCAA Convention in January 1986, Robinson was honored with the second special award ever given for coaching victories. The first, of course, went to Bryant.

"Nobody has ever done or will do what Eddie Robinson has done for this game," Paterno said. "Our profession will never, ever be able to repay Eddie Robinson for what he has done for the country and the profession of football."

Robinson also was Grambling's head basketball coach from 1942 to 1956, posting a record of 288-120, and served for a time as baseball coach as well. He coached the 1943 and 1944 seasons at Grambling High School when the college dropped football because of World War II. That's where he met Tank Younger, who later became the first player from a historically black school to be drafted by the National Football League. Robinson sent more than 300 players to professional football camps, and 200 or so made NFL rosters.

I first met Eddie Robinson about 30 years ago when the NCAA held its annual convention in Houston. Robinson was part of a panel discussing whether athletic scholarships should be based on need.

I don't recall who else was on the panel, but I clearly remember Robinson saying with a sly grin that he had never had a player whose chance to attend college didn't depend on need.

Robinson passed Bear Bryant and became college football's all-time winningest coach in a game against Texas Southern that was played in the Cotton Bowl in Dallas. I was accompanied by Denne Freeman, the Southwest regional sports editor for the Associated Press.

On Texas Southern's first play from scrimmage, the press box intercom blurted out the news, "Bro' drops back to pass."

Denne and I looked at each other and I said, "Are they going to call everyone Bro'?"

Turns out the Texas Southern quarterback was named Dennis Brow.

Like all coaches, Robinson could poor-mouth when he wanted to. Grambling invaded New York one year for its annual visit, and Robinson moaned about how small his team was.

The Grambling roster listed 10 offensive and defensive tackles and only one weighed less than 300 pounds.

Where it All Began

New Brunswick, N.J., November 6, 1869. Rutgers 6, Princeton 4.

That was the first "football" game ever played, and that's where I started covering college football some 92 years later. I "led" Rutgers to its first unbeaten season in 1961, but it wasn't easy.

In the finale, Rutgers trailed Columbia 19-6 in the fourth quarter. The Scarlet Knights scored to make it 19-12, and Coach John Bateman inexplicably ordered a two-point conversion. Bateman said later he misread the scoreboard.

All's well that ends well, and "we" won the game 32-19 to complete a 9-0 season.

Rutgers is a unique place. In the 1960s, it played a schedule mostly against teams from the Ivy League and schools that now belong to the Patriot League. All are now Division I-AA teams. Rutgers also doesn't have a school of physical education. It would be unkind to say that Rutgers doesn't have a football team, either. The Scarlet Knights won a game in 1999, beating Syracuse. I can vouch for it because I was there. That was one more than they won in 1997.

Division I-A teams like Penn State and Tennessee began showing up on the schedule in the late 1970s, only to be followed by a Bucknell or a William & Mary. Rutgers couldn't make up its mind what it wanted to be. The school was excellent academically, but not on a par with the Ivy League. Athletically, Rutgers was a shade below the Penn States, Pittsburghs and other Eastern powers.

Rutgers actually beat Tennessee in Knoxville 13-7 in 1979, dropped a 17-13 squeaker to Alabama in 1980 and tied Florida 28-28 in 1985, but not until 1986 did Division I-AA teams disappear from the schedule for the most part.

I have always believed that the name of the school is a drawback. Rutgers is the only university in the nation to have been a colonial college, a land-grant college and a state university. It also is the only state university that doesn't go by the name of its state, although the Rutgers Stadium end zone has a "New Jersey" logo and the helmets once carried an "N.J." on the side.

Rutgers was founded in 1766 as Queen's College and became Rutgers College in 1825, honoring Col. Henry Rutgers, a benefactor, a former trustee and a Revolutionary War veteran. It would be better off as the University of New Jersey.

In 1983, Rutgers fired Coach Frank Burns despite an overall 78-43-1 record and the school's only bowl game, a respectable 34-18 loss to Arizona State in the 1978 Garden State Bowl.

It's not generally known, but Rutgers, through the late Sonny Werblin, actually approached Joe Paterno before hiring Dick Anderson, a Penn State assistant in 1984. Anderson lasted six years, then was fired with a 27-34-4 record.

Enter Doug Graber, fresh from seven years as a respected defensive assistant in the NFL. Exit Graber, like Anderson, after six years, with a remarkably similar 29-36-1 record, although Anderson managed to beat Penn State and Michigan State in the same year. Graber didn't have a victory of that magnitude.

Despite almost 50,000 students on three campuses, a ranking as one of the nation's top 50 universities by *U.S. News & World Report* and membership in the Big East Conference, Rutgers remains an enigma. The official name is Rutgers, the State University. Can you name the state? Miami coach Butch Davis once told me many of his players can't.

"Occasionally we'll run into a kid in Florida, or someplace like that, who calls it Root-gers, or something like that," Graber once said.

In 1994, Graber spoke at the New York State High School All-Star Game in Rochester and was being driven to the airport by a hotel employee.

"He asked if I was the coach at Rutgers and I said yeah and he said, 'Who do you play? What conference is that in?' And there's Syracuse right down the road. We've only been playing them for 20 years. It's still kind of a misunderstood place in a lot of respects."

How about a name change?

"I think it's a moot point because I don't think it's ever gonna happen," Graber said before his departure. "We always have to answer a lot of questions right off the bat—where's that place anyway? I don't think there's ever been a university that's more misunderstood than Rutgers, and if you look at the history, you can see why. It's a university that's undergone dramatic and huge changes over the past 20 years, and that's the reason for it."

Rutgers is an hour or so south of New York City and not much farther north of Philadelphia. On the map, Rutgers is located in the center of New Jersey. On the college football map, it is located in the middle of nowhere. You have to go more than 200 miles to Penn State to find the nearest college football hotbed. New Jersey belongs to the Giants and Jets up north and the Eagles down south. Pro football dominates the sports pages.

Burns begged for better facilities. He didn't get them. Anderson did, but his recruiting left something to be desired. Graber got a new stadium, almost double the size of the old one, and kept some good home-grown players in the state.

When Graber was fired, I called Fred Gruninger, then the athletic director, to recommend Jack Bicknell, a former head coach at Boston College and a New Jersey native. Bicknell, I believed, would have united the high school coaches in New Jersey, which is important in a state that usually loses its best prospects to Penn State, Michigan, Ohio State, and the like. Bicknell actually applied for the job.

A few nights later, Gruninger called me.

"Do you know Glen Mason (then the Kansas coach)?" he asked. I said I did.

"Would you mind calling Mason to see if it's OK with him if we call his athletic director to request permission to speak to him?"

I did; Mason, another Jersey boy, said OK.

A few nights later, Gruninger called again.

"Do you know Bob Davie (then a Notre Dame assistant)?"

I said I had met Davie during his days as an assistant at Pittsburgh, but didn't really know him. I also told Gruninger that hiring someone from Notre Dame would take a few headlines away from the Giants and Jets, which is something Rutgers needed.

A few nights later, Gruninger called yet again.

"Do you know Terry Shea?"

I said I only knew Shea by reputation. Gruninger said Bill Walsh had recommended Shea and promised to speak at Rutgers' spring clinic if the school hired Shea. I said I thought that was a pretty weak reason to hire a coach, and I also wondered why Shea didn't get the Stanford job when Walsh left (He was offensive coordinator).

The new coach turned out to be Shea, who posted an 8-36 record in his first four seasons, including 0-11 in 1997, the school's first winless campaign since 1901. Rutgers rebounded with a 5-6 mark in 1998 and Shea was named Big East Coach of the Year.

It got so bad in 1997 that

—Prior to the televised Syracuse game, ESPN asked the Rutgers sports information office whether it should introduce the offense or the defense. "Just introduce the punter," was the sarcastic reply.

—In the final minutes, with Syracuse ahead 50-3, the Orangemen had the ball inside the Rutgers 10-yard line. The Syracuse quarterback further embarrassed the Scarlet Knights by taking a knee four straight times. There is nothing more humiliating than having the opposition not even try to score.

—As the remnants of the crowd filed out of Rutgers Stadium, the P.A. system reminded everyone to be sure and see the statue commemorating the birthplace of college football. "Yeah," snorted one disgruntled Rutgers fan, "it's a tombstone."

John Elway is synonymous with "The Drive."

I saw one that even Elway would have admired.

It took place on September 29, 1962, at Princeton's Palmer Stadium.

On the second play of the fourth quarter Rutgers punted to the Princeton 4-yard line. Princeton led 8-7 at the time. It was 15-7 when Rutgers got the ball back 20 plays, 96 yards and more than 10 minutes later.

This was how the drive looked in the official play-by-play:

1-10 P4 Riley off tackle.

2-3 P11 Riley around right end.

3-4 P10 Riley around left end, first down.

1-10 P14 Riley up middle.

2-5 P19 Merlini up middle, first down.

1-10 P25 Riley carries.

2-5 P30 Riley around right end.

3-1 P34 Merlini up middle, first down.

1-10 P36 Terpack around right end.

2-5 P41 Riley off tackle, first down.

1-10 P48 Riley through middle.

2-3 R47 Riley left end, first down.

1-10 R41 Merlini around left end, first down.

1-10 R25 Terpack left end.

2-4 R21 Merlini through middle.

3-2 R17 Merlini over middle, first down.

1-10 R14 Riley off tackle.

2-4 R8 Riley through middle for touchdown (offside penalty against Princeton).

2-9 R13 Riley up middle, first down.

1-2 R2 Merlini up middle.

2-1 Merlini up middle for TD at 10:27 of fourth quarter, Gouldin's kick for extra point is good.

Opinions

You're entitled to your opinions and I'm entitled to mine. Here are some of mine. If you want me to read yours, write a book:

—As far as working conditions go, the best press box I've ever been in is at West Virginia's Mountaineer Field.

—Isn't the ballyhooed West Coast Offense essentially the same thing LaVell Edwards has been running at Brigham Young for the last quarter century or so? And what Cactus Jack Curtice ran at Utah before that?

—Florida coach Steve Spurrier may be worth every penny of his $2 million-a-year contract. If so, what does that make Kansas State's Bill Snyder worth? Snyder has done probably the greatest coaching job in college football history in turning around the nation's worst program. The Wildcats were 300-511-39 when he took over in

Herschel Nissenson and LaVell Edwards
(Photo courtesy of Herschel Nissenson)

1989 (a .376 percentage) and have gone 55-36-1—.603 since.

—If there's a drawback to covering a Notre Dame-Michigan game, it's having to hear those two fight songs a hundred times apiece.

—The college celebration rule has got to go.

—Isn't it strange that every player drafted by the NFL "needs to work on his upper-body strength and his technique." What have they been doing in college besides pumping iron. And don't college coaches teach technique?

—Isn't it silly for a false-start penalty to be a deadball foul? All it does is penalize the defense for a big play.

—I have seen scores of marching bands over the years, and one thing has always puzzled me—why are there so many tuba players? Do you know anyone who grew up wanting to be a virtuoso on the tuba?

—If spiking the ball isn't intentional grounding, pray tell me what is?

—How come it's okay for an entire team to run out to home plate to congratulate a player who hits a home run during the College World Series, but running to the end zone to mob a player who scores a touchdown is a 15-yard penalty?

—When Gerry Faust was saying all those Hail Marys on the Notre Dame sideline, I always wanted to ask him what would happen if the other coach was saying them, too. My experience has always been that God favors the team with the bigger, stronger and faster players.

—Who'd have ever thought Notre Dame would become a basketball school—a women's basketball school.

"Tids"

"Tids" is a popular word at ESPN. It's short for tidbits. Producers are always asking for "tids"— interesting little nuggets of information. You, the reader, didn't ask, but I've decided to give you some anyway.

•••

Shortly after Watson Brown took over as head coach at Rice following the 1983 season, he received a call from an old friend, a high school coach named Donnie Laurence. They had coached together on Rex Dockery's staff at Texas Tech.

"Watson," Donnie Laurence said, "I've got a really good player who's being recruited by Baylor and Texas Tech and some different people, but you get in here and you've got a shot at him. Get on down here and see him right away."

The player was a lineman, so Brown sent Mark Bradley, his line coach, to scout the kid. When Brown said Taylor High School, Bradley looked at the map and took off for Taylor, Texas, which is just outside of Austin, a fur piece from Rice.

Bradley reported (1) that the coach there—he took for granted that it was Donnie Laurence—looked at him kind of funny, and (2) the player weighed around 200 pounds and couldn't play, not even for Rice. Brown told him to come home.

A week or so later, Donnie Laurence called Brown again.

"Watson." he said, "dang, I told you I've got a player. We're right down the road from you. Why didn't you have a guy here?"

"He's been there," Brown said. "He talked to you."

"Ain't been no coach talking to me," Laurence said.

That's when Brown found out Bradley had gone to Taylor, Texas, instead of Taylor High School in Katy, a Houston suburb.

Army used to hold its annual preseason media day in late summer at a retreat called Bull Pond, a place where officers went for R&R. It was part of the Military Academy reservation, but in the hills and wilderness about 10 miles from the main campus.

Fred Russell was invited one year and Bill Battle picked him up at the airport. To get to Bull Pond you must take a mountain road for a mile or so up into the hills.

When they got to the bottom of said road, Battle told Russell, "Fred, I'm late for a meeting but they know you're here. Just wait for a minute and someone will come to pick you up."

Fred Russell, the epitome of a Southern gentleman, got out and waited by the side of the road, dressed to the nines and carrying his suitcase.

There is a large open field there. Suddenly, puffs of white smoke began rising accompanied by sounds of exploding shells. A voice came over a loudspeaker, "Clear the artillery range. You are in a live artillery range."

Naturally, the coaching staff was hiding behind some trees watching the action and laughing their heads off. Someone somewhere still has the film of Russell diving head over heels into a roadside ditch.

By the way, if you've watched Lee Corso predict the outcome of games, you'll notice that when he forecasts an ESPN game, he holds his thumb and forefinger an inch or so apart and says it will be decided by a field goal in the fourth quarter.

ESPN told him never to predict a blowout on an ESPN game. That could cause some folks not to watch.

Coach Billy Joe of Central State (Ohio), a former president of the American Football Coaches Association, once was told by a fellow coach, a good ol' boy, reportedly from Texas, "Where I come from, we got a lotta folks named Billy Joe, but most of 'em got last names."

The two greatest golf shots I ever saw were struck by football coaches.

The 15th hole at the Stillwater (Oklahoma) Country Club is a par 5. The fairway runs past a huge wooded area on the right. If your drive gets past the trees, your second shot must clear a small pond.

I saw Jimmy Johnson take a mulligan after his second shot drowned. The mulligan cleared the trees, cleared the water, hit the green and stopped at the edge of the hole for a tap-in eagle.

Jim Sweeney, who finished his career by building Fresno State into a west coast power, and I were in the same foursome at a scramble on the Cottonwood Valley course in Irving, Texas.

Our best tee shot on one of the par 5s was in the fairway by a foot or so. The rest of the hole was uphill and you could barely see the flag, much less the green. Sweeney knew his rules.

"I can move the ball two club lengths," he said. "I'm going to move it into the rough so I can hit my driver."

He did and smacked the ball within a foot of the hole. Another tap-in eagle.

Johnny Majors was in his second stint at the University of Pittsburgh in 1996, when Memphis State upset Tennessee 21-17.

Tennessee was Majors' alma mater, but the school had fired him a few years earlier, so this upset didn't upset him.

He called me a few days later.

"Can you tell me the score of the Memphis State-Tennessee game?" he said. "I can't find it anywhere."

"Come off it, John," I said.

"No, no," he insisted. "I can't find it."

"Believe it or not," I said, "Memphis State won 21-17."

"That explains it," Majors said.

"Explains what?" I asked.

"My whole family was upset all weekend," he said. "My brother was upset, my brother-in-law was upset."

Besides Florida State's streak of 13 straight 10-win seasons and the same number of consecutive top 10 finishes, there are two other remarkable college football feats.

—Nebraska has won at least nine games for 31 straight years.

—Robert R. Neyland served three stints as head coach at Tennessee around military service. Neyland coached a total of 216 games, and Tennessee shut out its opponent in 112 of them.

Every time I hear someone complain about the rankings, I recall that Duke in 1938 and Tennessee in 1939 were unbeaten, untied *and unscored upon*—and neither team won the national championship?

Gerry DiNardo was born and raised in Brooklyn, New York, went to prep school in Massachusetts, then to Notre Dame and coached at Maine, Eastern Michigan and Colorado before traveling below the Mason-Dixon line to become head coach at Vanderbilt in 1991.

DiNardo said he was so naive when he first headed south that he went into a restaurant and ordered chicken-fried steak "medium well."

When Bill Battle coached his last game for Tennessee in 1976 (against Vanderbilt in Nashville), the head linesman was Bobby Gaston, now the Southeastern Conference's supervisor of officials.

During a lull late in the game, Gaston wandered over to wish Battle good luck in his future endeavors and to tell him the officials appreciated the way Battle always got along with them. Unfortunately, he picked a day when Battle wasn't thrilled with the officiating.

"You have a funny way of showing it," he said.

Any doubts I may have had that Kentucky is a basketball school were eliminated one May when I called then-SID Russell Rice.

Tales from College Football's Sidelines

"I'm sorry," the secretary said (They still had live people answering phones in those days), "he's at basketball practice."

"In May?" I said.

"Oh, I'm sorry, I mean football practice," she said.

"Don't worry," I replied. "I know the way you people think."

So when Kentucky hired Hal Mumme as its new football coach, the following gag got started: "You know where Kentucky's athletic priorities lie. When they needed a basketball coach, they went to the New York Knicks (Rick Pitino); when they needed a football coach, they went to Valdosta State (Mumme)."

Baylor beat Tennessee 13-7 in the January 1, 1957, Sugar Bowl.

The key play occurred when Tennessee's great Johnny Majors, who had finished second in the Heisman Trophy voting, fumbled a punt at his 15-yard line to set up Baylor's winning touchdown.

A short time later, some Tennessee players participated in the opening of a supermarket and Majors was handed a baby to pose with. The baby's disgruntled father was heard to mutter, "I hope he doesn't fumble the kid."

224

While the Gator Bowl was being renovated in 1994-95, Florida and Georgia played "The World's Largest Outdoor Cocktail Party" home-and-home.

The 1994 game was played in Gainesville, and Florida won handily 52-14. The next year the scene shifted to Athens. Florida was ahead 45-17 in the closing minutes and had the ball on the Georgia 8-yard line. Coach Steve Spurrier sent in the field goal unit.

Before the kick could be attempted, someone phoned down to Spurrier from the press box that no one had ever scored 50 points against Georgia in Sanford Stadium.

Spurrier's hands went up in the time-honored time-out signal.

Off came the field goal team, in came a pass play. It was successful—Eric Kresser to Travis McGriff—and it marked the first time Georgia had surrendered 50 points between the hedges.

"Have now," came Spurrier's cackle through the phone lines.

All's fair in love, war . . . and recruiting.

Several decades ago, many schools were lusting after a promising Polish high school placekicker named Chester Marcol, who didn't speak much English.

Duffy Daugherty couldn't get him into Michigan State because of a foreign language requirement. So

Muddy Waters signed him for tiny Hillsdale College by making English a foreign language for Marcol.

⬤

The most unbelievable way I ever saw to lose a football occurred in the 1968 Ivy League contest between Harvard and Columbia.

Harvard punted deep into Columbia territory, and players from both sides circled around and watched the bouncing pigskin. Suddenly, a Columbia player reached in and downed the ball—or so he thought.

Since the Lions were the receiving team, that made it a fumble. Harvard recovered and scored the winning touchdown (21-14) a few plays later.

⬤

If Joe Paterno ever decides to leave Penn State, there's a chair with his name on it at Brown University.

Not that JoePa will ever coach at his alma mater. After all, the man is in his 70s, and State College, Pennsylvania, has been his home for more than half a century.

But the first athletic chair ever established at Brown —these are pretty common in the Ivy League—is called the Howard D. Williams '17/Joseph V. Paterno '50 Football Coaching Chair.

It was established by Roger D. Williams, Brown's 1945 captain, with a gift of $1 million in honor of his father and Paterno, who lettered in 1947-48-49, co-captained the '49 club and still shares the school's career record for interceptions with 14. In addition to playing defensive back, Paterno quarterbacked the '49 team, considered to be Brown's finest. Paterno didn't give any money for the coaching chair, which isn't unusual; it was merely named in his honor.

Payne Stewart's plane flew westward from Orlando, headed for Texas and a golf tournament; Bo Rein's plane flew eastward from Shreveport, Louisiana, headed across the state for Baton Rouge and his new home after a recruiting trip.

Payne Stewart's Learjet cruised for 1,400 miles before crashing in a field in South Dakota, where the only witnesses were cows; Bo Rein's Cessna 411 Conquest twin turboprop flew in a straight line—but off course—for hundreds of miles before spinning out of control and plunging into the Atlantic Ocean 100 miles off the Virginia coast.

The weather and visibility were poor, waves were several feet high and the water temperature was 40 degrees. The ocean was 1,100 feet deep.

The mystery of Bo Rein's plane has never been solved. It was, in fact, declared unsolvable by the National Transportation Safety Board.

Rein was 34 years old, one of the nation's bright young coaches, when his plane went down on Jan. 10, 1980, little more than a month after he was named head coach at Louisiana State University following four years at North Carolina State, where he had a 27-18-1 record and took the Wolfpack to two bowl games.

A graduate of Ohio University, Rein played three seasons of minor league baseball in the Cleveland Indians chain before an Achilles tendon injury ended his career. He was drafted by the NFL's Baltimore Colts, but never played pro football.

Rein was the only passenger aboard a plane piloted by Louis Benscotter, 47, a veteran flier. Shortly after take-off, Benscotter was advised of heavy thunderstorms in the Baton Rouge area. He received permission to head for Jackson, Mississippi. There was no further radio contact.

Barely 16 minutes after takeoff, too soon for the aircraft to be at an oxygen-free altitude, the FAA lost radio contact with the plane. The captain of a Pan Am flight in the area said he heard Benscotter trying to respond to Fort Worth Air Traffic Control, but the transmission was weak.

In both cases, fighter planes chased the runaway aircraft, but there was nothing they could do except keep other planes out of the way. Air Force Capt. Daniel Zoerb, flying in an F-106 fighter out of Langley Air Force Base in Virginia, said he saw no sign of life aboard Rein's plane, only a red glow, probably from the plane's instrument panel.

A puzzling aspect was that none of the pilots chasing Rein's plane could see anyone on board. If Benscotter was unconscious in his seat, the weight of his feet and legs would have affected the plane's course. Instead, it climbed slowly, agonizingly, to more than 40,000 feet before apparently running out of fuel.

The cabin was pressurized and the plane had an elaborate safety system, including warning lights and horns when it reached dangerous heights without the pressurization system. The plane was a relatively new one and had passed all safety checks.

Whatever happened to Rein and Benscotter happened within minutes after takeoff. What it was we'll never know. The NTSB considered oxygen deprivation, along with numerous other possibilities, but never arrived at an absolute determination. Almost a year after the crash, the NTSB said it was "unable to determine a cause because it was unable to find any wreckage."

The late Dick Colman, who coached Princeton from 1957 to 1968, used to say, "Yalies are bad enough when they're losing, but when they're winning they're absolutely insufferable."

Modesty prevents me from tooting my own horn, so I will quote from the *Huntsville* (Alabama) *Times* of April 15, 1979, reporting on Alabama's spring game the previous day at Tuscaloosa's Bryant-Denny Stadium:

> Herschel Nissenson, the Associated Press' College Football Editor, presented the Crimson Tide with the wire service's official trophy for the (1978) national title.
>
> Nissenson accomplished a rare feat for a sports writer when he drew a roaring ovation for his speech before presenting the trophy. Crowd pleasers like "We're giving you a new trophy because we knew you wouldn't want the same one as Notre Dame" and "Thank you for all your bumper stickers from last year saying 'AP No. 2, Alabama No. 1,' earned approval from the 7,500 fans in attendance.
>
> Nissenson concluded his remarks by saying, "We're not afraid to correct our mistake (awarding the 1977 national championship to Notre Dame). Here's to the No. 1 football team in the nation."